CONTENTS

Published by:
Heinerth Productions Inc.
5989 NE County Road 340, High Springs, Fl 32643 USA
First published 2014 © Robert McClellan

Book design by Heinerth Productions Inc.
www.IntoThePlanet.com • www.RobertMcClellan.com
Printed in the USA   ISBN 978-1-940944-03-6

DISCUSSION
BOOK CLUB
SELECTION

BOOM
BABY
BOOM

VOLUME 1

ROBERT McCLELLAN

A Baby Boomer's Tales of
Sex, Drugs, Rock & Roll and Recovery

BOOM BABY BOOM
VOLUME 1

A Baby Boomer's Tales of
Sex, Drugs, Rock & Roll and Recovery

Robert McClellan

ABOUT THE AUTHOR

Robert McClellan has been at various times, a concert stage manager, a combat photographer, a Navy Seabee, a truck driver, an alcoholic, a real estate agent, a radio talk show host, a filmmaker, a prison nurse, and a less than perfect husband and father.

Robert lives in Florida with his underwater explorer wife Jill Heinerth, with whom he recently rode his bicycle across Canada. With Boom Baby Boom, Robert shares a colorful selection of essays and short stories.

Be the first to access exclusive new content at:
www.RobertMcClellan.com

AUTHOR'S STATEMENT

These essays consist of absolutely true, almost true, and completely embellished elements. It is not my intent to embarrass or demean anyone, other than myself, in this work. Therefore I have chosen to partially fictionalize some characters, change some names, and alter various details to protect people for whom I care greatly.

ACKNOWLEDGMENT

*Every once in a while, the Universe conspires to
bring two beings together that were meant
to share the light of all Eternity.*

*To my wife, partner, and best friend Jill,
I express the utmost gratitude for
saving me from myself.*

And listening without prejudice.

I WANT MY JETPACK

As a young boy I was promised a future with General Electric jet packs and Lockheed personal sport helicopters to whisk me around the neighborhood. I looked forward to a synthetic-skinned robotic house keeper who, without the slightest complaint, would pick up and launder my dirty socks and underwear. I eagerly anticipated popping magic yellow nutrition pills for breakfast, and sucking on high octane energy gels that tasted like coffee and chocolate. My boss would be a jovial, caring mentor and my assigned soulmate would be a sultry Amazon siren, straight from a Russ Meyer movie.

The twenty-first century would be the first where humans no longer labored; we'd work from our intelligent, autonomous nuclear powered homes for a few hours a day, then hop on a supersonic intercontinental shuttle to jet ski the afternoon away, skimming like graceful gulls across an ancient African lake. Life would be the perfect balance of meaningful work and invigorating leisure.

By now, I expected a cooperative society made up of happy engineers, scientists and artists. I would remotely operate giant lunar mining equipment from my lounge chair console, built into the luxury kevlar pods of my wireless home office. Great virtual works of art would hover like giant holograms above my verdant, green garden space. Music would float in the ether, accessed by an embedded chip located just behind my left ear.

I'd swirl through the great classics, or dance to the latest techno bop, delivered subconsciously through invisible aural receptors.

In my fantasy future healthcare and all basic human needs would be equally provided to everyone. War would be obsolete. We'd all belong to the same prosperous culture, the same happy sameness. There would be no nation states or religions. We'd all live a comfortable, actualized existence, brought to you by PepsiCo, Honda, and Pfizer.

Maybe I expected too much.

I was raised to believe anything was possible. My potential was limitless and I was infinitely optimistic. If I worked hard I was promised a peaceful and creative culture, where socio-economic classes, sex, race and ethnicity were antiquated stereotypes from a more vulgar time. Technology and science would save me from myself, and I'd tap into the new enlightenment, a silicon based spirituality.

It really should have been better.

Life for the middle class in America wasn't supposed to be like this.

This hard.

This mean.

This fearful.

This greedy.

This unjust.

This fraudulent.

This dysfunctionally corrupt.

This way.

EPIPHANY

I am cold and smell like stale beer and anger.

My younger daughter, Lilly, has climbed onto my chest and is happily snoozing away. She is warm and smells like Heaven.

I am laying, hungover again, on the big brown sofa in the living room. My tiny daughter is nestled up with me, taking a well-deserved nap. She spent most of the morning joyfully tearing open a modest pile of Christmas presents.

I missed it.

On Christmas Eve, I took the last of the money that my wife had saved for some big presents for our two girls, and spent it drinking and partying in the bars and strip joints of Pensacola. The last place I consciously remember being was Trader Jon's, the legendary Navy tavern on Palafox Street. I woke up at 5 a.m. on Christmas morning, splayed out on the stinky carpet of some tattooed biker chick's apartment, with her smelly Dachshund puppy licking the vomit from my shirt.

Blackout. Again.

This is it. I never want to feel as bad as I do right now. I don't want my girls to be disappointed and embarrassed by their stupid, drunken father.

I can no longer live this way.

There are only two choices; kill myself or get sober.

With Lilly on my chest, and older daughter Zoey nuzzled up in the crook of my arm, in this very instant of life or death, I have my moment of sudden revelation and insight. I choose life.

I must find a way to get sober.

Over twenty years have passed. My relationship with my daughters has waxed and waned. Although I've been absent for most of the significant events of their lives, they have forgiven me. We have embarked on a new path of discovery and acceptance. My long inventory of character defects can never be excused, and, thankfully, my adult daughters have no desire to dredge up the insults of the past. Instead, they love me for the man I am today. I am humbled and grateful.

Today is December 27.

Yesterday, I marked my 23rd year in recovery. I am in my Lilly's warm house on a cold Philadelphia afternoon, with her boy Noah, my grandson, fidgeting on my lap.

He is warm and smells like forgiveness.

IT WASN'T SUPPOSED TO BE LIKE THIS

We are secretly dark men. The light of our expectations has dimmed. Hating ourselves while taking long drags on unfiltered Camels, we are miserable. Born into the most prosperous and dynamic generation in history, we pissed much of our potential away.

Our superficial mantra is "he who dies with the most toys wins."

To this end, we shine custom chromed Harley's in three car garages as our post-menopausal wives open the mail and find another overdue credit card bill. Now, in our fifties and sixties, we watch apathetically as Wrangler waistlines expand and 401K balances contract. We bitterly march in Tea Party formations, railing against this week's imaginary enemy. We medicate our sallow-skinned children into submission, and anesthetize our unfulfilled American dreams with designer vodka and micro-brewed hipster ale.

It wasn't supposed to be like this.

You have seen us around. Marching like lemmings into big box home centers, we try to connect with our self reliant ancestry. Using hand tools, our grandfather's built their own houses, but we need a cordless hammer drill and a laser level to hang a picture frame in our daughter's room.

We are the sons of the "Greatest Generation." Our parents built the most advanced and prosperous society in history. And gave it to us.

Born after the Second World War, and coming of age in the "Happy Days" of the nineteen fifties and sixties, we Boomers were baptized in the holy waters of optimism.

We would land a man on the moon and invent the Internet. We discovered Ray Charles and birthed the Beatles. Together, we fought for civil rights and elected the first Black president. Dutifully, we went to Vietnam, and today, we reluctantly send our kids to the killing fields of Iraq and Afghanistan. We cheered as USA Hockey won Olympic gold; and in the arms of strangers, we cried in horror as the Twin Towers fell.

We are simultaneously the best and the worst that America produces. An enigma, enveloped in a generational contradiction. We build and destroy with impunity. On our way to meet our buddies at the sports bar, we callously step around the homeless man, never considering that we are only a few drinks away from the same fate.

For our penance, on the weekend we wear pink ball caps and slog through our wive's breast cancer charity walk. We take our kids to soccer and ice cream, and continue the farce that all is well in our little deed restricted world.

It wasn't supposed to be like this.

VIETNAM

Billy Shay was the fastest white boy in Olney. He was tall and thin and looked like a gazelle. The high school track coach tried in vain to get Billy on the cross-country team. He didn't like school and he didn't like teams.

He just liked to run.

Once in a while, Billy, who was about five years older than me, would play touch football on the street with us younger guys. There was only one play: throw the ball as far as you could and Billy would run under it for a touchdown. He could have scored on every down. He had just gotten a job with the post office and bought a brand new dark blue Pontiac GTO. Billy had long, dark, curly hair and his sly smile had the corner girl's attention every time he pulled up in that rumbling muscle car. He was drafted into the Army a few months after he turned nineteen. He went to Vietnam.

Billy's younger sister Susan was the most beautiful girl on our street. She had long blonde hair and the softest blue eyes I'd ever seen. When she smiled and said hello to me, I'd melt right into the pavement. We'd sneak up the alley when she was on the back porch sunbathing in her bikini to get a glimpse of her. She dated another older guy named Steve, who was studying to be a teacher. Steve had a draft deferment because he was in college. He was a good guy who played baseball for

Temple University, and helped take them to the college World Series. He and Billy and Susan were the best looking and most popular young people around.

I was in the corner store buying a cream soda on a hot summer afternoon when the lady behind the counter, Mrs. Angelo, dropped the black telephone on the floor and began wailing, crying, screaming, trembling and praying in Italian. "What's the use…what's the use… Why? Why…?"

I tried to pay for the soda but she kept saying, "What's the use?" interspersed with Italian words I couldn't understand. She came out from behind the counter and grabbed my arm. She was a little woman, but had a strong grip on me. She squeezed harder and harder saying in broken English, "Take them all… No!"…She looked me in the eye and said, "They take our Billy!… Our Billy…They can have no more!… No…No more…!"

By the time I wrestled free of the distraught Mrs. Angelo and escaped back out to the street, the neighborhood was hysterical. There were mothers and daughters running to the Shay's house. Old ladies were on the porch steps sobbing. The tough working men who had stopped in to McGinty's bar down the street were standing outside, holding bottles of beer and staring silently down at their shoes.

A taxi pulled up in front of the house and from the back seat exited Mr. Shay, Billy and Susan's dad. The driver got out and stood quietly next to his cab smoking a cigarette. Mr. Shay was in his brown work overalls from the plant where he was a foreman. He was a tall man and he towered over the women lining the sidewalk. He said nothing, made contact with no one and disappeared into the house.

A long gray Buick slowly turned the corner and parked on the pavement across from the house. Out stepped Father Graham, from Saint Helena's. The Shay's went to public school and I didn't know they were Catholic. The older women faced the priest and made the sign of the cross as he walked past, blessing them.

My friends Joey and Fran Hurley ran up to me.

"Billy Shay got killed!"

"Holy shit!"

"They said he knifed the 'Cong that shot him!"

Then I saw my father.

He walked over to me and Joey and Fran. It was two in the afternoon on a weekday and the only other time my dad came home early from work was the day Kennedy was assassinated. My father, a strong, tall, red-headed Scotsman, reached over and put one big arm around my neck and wrapped the two Hurley boys in the other.

"Let's go, lads. Your mother's will be wanting you near today."

Susan and Steve broke up and I never saw her blue eyes smiling again.

The war in Vietnam raged on.

I registered for the draft on my eighteenth birthday.

LOVE AT FIRST

I can hear her walking around upstairs.

She wears jingle bells on her shoes.

I wait on the basement sofa for her to return.

She comes down the steep set of stairs and dances toward me smiling. She has big, wet, saucer-shaped brown eyes and wavy shoulder length black hair. Her athletic, thin body is slightly curved at her hips and she has small firm breasts, tightly wrapped in a yellow halter blouse. Her faded jeans have red stitching and could have been painted on. She wears a thin, glittered plastic belt, which she is unbuckling as she slides down beside me on the old couch.

"My mom's asleep and my sister's still at school," she whispers as she places my hand between her thighs.

I feel every anticipatory breath she takes as I slide my hand inside her panties and feel the soft wetness of Krista.

She smiles, closes her eyes and kisses me deeply as she lowers her body, pulling me down with her to a laying position. Krista is unbuttoning my jeans and reaching her small, soft hand into my fly.

I can hear every sensual note of Jim Morrison's "L.A. Woman" on the turntable:

" Are you a lucky little lady in the city of light,
Or just another lost angel...? "

We probe and stroke and caress and quiver and lick and suck and explode together.

We are fifteen years old and we are in love.

NOVEMBER '63

1.

The steam heat in the crowded classroom is not turned on yet for the winter. I'm wearing a navy cardigan sweater over my light blue school shirt and my official Archdiocese of Philadelphia clip-on tie. The sweater is about two inches thick, a hand me down from my mother's step-brother Jim. I can't bring myself to call him "Uncle" because he is only two grades ahead of me. I am practically swimming in the scratchy wool sweater and have cuffed the sleeves up three times to access my boney hands. I've chewed my fingernails into sharp, uneven shards and they keep getting caught in the loose threads of the cardigan.

The top half of my body is toasty, and I'm bordering on breaking into a November sweat. A thin slice of sun streams through the arched Catholic school windows. I get lost in the tiny, floating specks of chalk dust that dance through the beam as it bears down on my little desk. I sit in the first aisle on the "St. Joseph's" side of the room. The boys are seated furthest from the doors to the right of Sister James' heavy oak desk. There is a double aisle separating us, the perilous, penis endowed, impure six-year old boys, from the treasured chastity of the innocent virgin girls in our classroom. The oversized aisle is a great line of demarcation, a flawlessly waxed zone of carefully-measured green tiled virtue. The territory is an uncorrupted No Man's Land where only adult staff members may tread. The other side of the room, to Sister's left, beyond the venereal demarcation, is where the girls sit with pleated skirts falling below their skinny kneecaps. This is the "Blessed Mother's" half of the class. This regimented segregation is crucial to saving us from our sinful first-grade impulses.

My face is hot but my ass is freezing. Although the sweater is more than adequate topside, the thin black dress pants I'm wearing are not a match for the cold wood and steel of my torturous schoolroom desk. My thin skivvies don't provide much insulation either. I rhythmically rock my legs, shaking and shimmying, in an attempt to warm them up. I also have to pee.

My rocking and rolling attracts Sister's unwelcome attention.

"Mr. McClellan!" she sharply screeches my name, "Why are you dancing like a Watusi?"

"Have you no self control?"

Popping to attention beside my desk, I meekly respond "Yes, sister, I mean no sister, I mean...I am cold sister."

"You can't be cold with that sweater, Mr. McClellan. Look around, most of the other boys don't have a sweater on at all, and they seem to be able to sit still in their seats!" She says, "Your problem little sir, is that you have no self control. Now, go stand in back for the rest of the period, and see if you can control yourself."

Embarrassed and self conscious, I drop my eyes to the floor and slowly trudge to the back of the class.

Sister calls out, "Face the corner and pray for self control young man."

I have two corners to choose from, and I head to the Blessed Mother's side, over by the back door.

This was apparently a serious breach in classroom decorum. Sister bolts down the center aisle, grabs me by my ear and leads me over to the St. Joe's corner, smashing my face into the heavy decorative trim where the walls meet. The hardwood scratches my cheek and I feel warm blood pulsing inside my lip.

Leaning down to my face, she chants "Self control, Robert, pray to your patron saint for self control!" In her starched black and white habit, and severe, thick soled nun boots, she seems eight feet tall.

I sniff and snort, but not a tear falls. I was not comfortable being physically assaulted by anyone, and I had already been in a few fist fights on the street when someone got too rough with me. I wanted to ball up my fist and pop Sister James right between the tits, but knew I'd get an ass whipping from my father for such a sacrilegious act as punching a Bride of Christ. Only fear of my dad coming down hard on me kept me from cold cocking her right in the aisle.

I mumble through a split lip, "Yes sister, I'm sorry sister, yes sister," and I taste rage.

But, even at six years of age, I knew better than to cry. To cry would be a victory for sister, and I'd be ashamed to face my friends on the street. "Crybaby" was one of he worst names that could be hung around a young boy's neck in this neighborhood.

I guess I learned something about self control after all. But I still had to piss.

Standing in the corner, with my hands folded in front of me, in a fake prayer pose, I peek out the window, studying the pigeons in the school yard. Most of them are a nondescript gray color with black trim, and an occasional greenish tint to their necks when the sun hits them at the right angle. They share scraps of food, and don't seem to fight or practice any violence at all. Among the ugly black ones were some pigeons that were light brown and white, prettier and much healthier looking. As the class drones on behind me, learning about Spot, Dick and Jane, I imagine myself flying to the rooftops with my new pigeon friends. Sucking at my torn inner lip, I enjoy the metallic taste of my own blood, and decide to be a pigeon for the rest of the morning.

The lunch bell rings, and Sister James tells me to join the line of children going home for lunch. I purposefully pass up the opportunity to use the boy's room, and made sure sister saw me skip right past it. I pissed in the alley behind the schoolyard.

2.

I meet my older sister Janice across the street, where she waits for me every day. I resent having to walk the three blocks to and from school with her, and especially having to hold her hand as we walk across the busiest intersections. I squeeze her hand halfway across, making her loosen her grip, and I bolt across without her. It is a miracle that I am never hit by a turning bus or distracted driver. I am no longer a baby and remind her every day. She is almost ten, and I am just six years old, but will soon be seven, and I put her on notice that I will no longer hold anyone's hand once I hit that milestone.

It is a sunny November day, and I run most of the way home. I don't give Jan a chance to get a good look at my cut lip. When my mother asks me about it, I tell her I ran into the fence during recess. I am always running into something, so this is hardly an unbelievable stretch. There is a code of silence about physical discipline from the nuns. If we make a big deal of it, our parents will often punish us more severely than the Sisters did. They figure we did something to deserve a whack from the nuns, and give us a licking to prompt us to mind our manners with the Holy Feminine Order. We Catholic kids are screwed.

After grilled cheese sandwiches and some ice on my lip, I am good to go.

3.

The early afternoon class starts with an hour of penmanship. We already know how to print, but now we are exploring the uncharted waters of the cursive Palmer Method. Up and down, flowing in tight circles, and loose curves, it is a fun class and a great foundation for a future as a graffiti artist.

Suddenly, the beeping intercom above the American flag interrupts our squiggles. It is Mother Superior's authoritative voice crackling through the ancient speakers: "All teachers and staff, please quietly enter the hallway outside your classrooms." That was it. A very cryptic order that I have never heard before. We are accustomed to the duck and cover air raid drills, where we crawled under our desks in case the Russians decided to bomb North Philadelphia. But this is different. No one is telling us to hit the deck, or walk outside to the fire drill meeting post in an orderly fashion. We all look at each other as sister immediately escapes to the hall. On the way out, she pivots, pokes her gnarly finger into the shoulder of Marie Ranieri, the teacher's pet who sits in the first desk, first row, and says, "Miss Ranieri will be taking names!" Marie is as startled as the rest of us, but she quickly pops open a copy book, wheels around in her seat and picks up her pencil. It looks like she is more than willing to snitch for Sister. I feel her unmerciful eyes on me and just continue my handwriting practice, head down and sitting up straight, both feet on the floor.

After a few minutes some voices are audible through the doors. The adults are all talking in that fake whisper-but-really-loud voice, and it doesn't sound like good news. The door opens slowly, and Sister James has a tissue to her eyes. Saying nothing, she walks over to her desk and sits down, clearing her throat.

"Children," she says, "put down your pencils and close your workbooks, please."

Wow, sister never says please.

"We will all kneel beside our desks."

This is the serious praying position for first-graders. Someone must be sick, or having an operation in the hospital. We kneel in straight rows, like little angels, hands clasped, fingers pointed toward heaven.

Sister, in a startling moment, hikes up her long, heavy black habit, and drops to her knees as well. She begins by saying "Hail Mary, full of grace, The Lord is with thee…" We all chime in now, just like a chorus, "Blessed art thou amongst women…" In sing-song voices we pray like good little Catholic kids. We do not know what, or who we are praying for, but the moment seemed pretty somber, so we just follow sister's lead through three Hail Mary's and an Our Father.

Sister stands and orders us to take our seats. The silence is eerie. Then the intercom crackles again, louder than before and, once more, it is Mother Superior. "All teachers, staff and children," she echoed through the schoolhouse, "we have asked for your prayers to be lifted to Heaven, in the arms of our Lord Jesus, for the benefit of our beloved President Kennedy, who was shot a few minutes ago in Texas. School will be dismissed at 3 o'clock and you are to go home immediately. If your parents are not presently at home, you are to report to Brother Rogers at the back pews of the upper church, where he will lead you and say the rosary. God bless America, and may Jesus Christ save his son, our President Kennedy."

Holy shit! The president has been shot! Our president. Our Roman Catholic, Irish president. He belonged to us and now someone is trying to take him!

There is no stopping the chatter and the crying and sobbing from everyone in the school. Kids, lay teachers, nuns, brothers and priests are all walking around like zombies. Finally, I find Janice in the schoolyard and grab her hand. She is crying, but I am in shock. I don't really know what to do, so I just hold her hand all the way home.

4.

By the time we make it onto Bonsall Street, the adults are waiting for all of us kids. Moms and aunts, and a few men too, swoop down on their children and whisk them into their houses. My mom is waiting on the front stoop. "Get in here Bobby," she said, "Just because you are home early does not mean you are going out to run the streets." That was it. No care or concern. No attempt to ease my anxiety about an event I do not comprehend, just a stern order - a warning that I am on a shorter leash than usual.

The big brown Philco television in the corner of the living room is on and the volume is turned up very loud. Aunt Linda, my mom's younger sister, is on the couch with a whiskey sour in her hand. Linda is our babysitter and barely old enough to drink. This is really unfamiliar territory for me. Obviously, something important is happening and the grown-ups are coming a little unglued. I try to ask Aunt Linda what is happening, but she and my mother just keep "hushing and shhhh'ussing" me, so I sit down next to Jan on the thick, floral carpet in front of the TV and try to follow along. Our little sister Theresa is upstairs taking a nap, oblivious to all of this in her candy-coated four year old dreams.

All three channels are broadcasting bulletins and special reports. Overwrought newsmen with microphones and headsets are getting teletype wires shoved in front of them every few seconds. They are agitatedly bouncing from one tiny bit of information to another, trying to piece together the events in Dallas. President Kennedy has been shot and killed.

Now, they are summarizing and reporting and speculating, in real time, and most of them seem pretty upset that a lot of what they are reporting can not be verified. I keep hoping they will get off the television so I can watch my usual after school reruns of Popeye and Superman. One of the good things that happened in the confusion of early dismissal was that Sister James forgot to put any homework on the blackboard, so, for the first time since school started, I don't have any weekend assignments.

Our phone keeps ringing and my mom runs into the kitchen to answer it. We have a party line with my aunt Nancy up the street, so between the two of them, it is non-stop phone calls as all the cousins, aunts and uncles check in with one another. Then, an hour and a half early, my father comes through the door, home from work.

On Fridays, My dad usually does the cooking. It was something he liked, and it was always a fun surprise dish. He'd make some exotic Asian noodle-ly thing, or just plain silly suppers like peanut butter omelets with potato chips and kosher pickles on the side. After supper, he'd go out with some of the other men on the block, and have a few beers and shoot darts, while my mom went grocery shopping at the Acme market around the corner. Fridays were paydays, and Friday nights were pretty special in our house. Janice and I got to stay up late, sometimes until ten or eleven o'clock, and Aunt Linda would sit with us.

Dad doesn't look like he is very interested in making supper. He pours a beer into a glass and plops down into his big chair. Dad is generally quiet, but so far, he has been home for fifteen minutes and has said almost nothing. I break the silence.

"Daddy, the Sisters let us come home early today," I say, while staring at the big screen three feet in front of my face. "We had to pray for President Kennedy."

He leans forward in his chair and says, "That's good son, prayers are a good thing right now." He lets out a huge sigh and sinks back into the cushions. On the wall above his chair is a crucifix, and some framed pictures of the pope and JFK at his inauguration.

With a progressive pope and a bright young president, Roman Catholic Americans, my father included, were feeling optimistic and empowered. Now, it is crashing down, and the men on the TV are full of unhappy, uncertain news.

Mom and Linda make bologna and cheese sandwiches and we stay glued to the television throughout the early evening. The latest word is that the police think they have found the guy who shot Kennedy. Our family routine is completely on hold. I am not sure what I am supposed to be doing, so I just hang out in the vicinity of my father, run to the kitchen to get him fresh beers when he asks, and try to understand at least half of what is going on. I am getting antsy, so my mom announces that bedtime is going to be 8 p.m., just like a school night, because the adults needed to talk.

Then it happens.

My father, the champion of strength in our family, grabs his big, blue work handkerchief from his back pocket and begins sobbing into it. At first, he tries to be subtle, but after a few moments, he just breaks down, burying his face and weeping. I have never seen my hero cry. It makes me sad too, and I start to well up and sniffle. Trying to not stare at him, but also totally engaged in his sadness, I do not say anything. Janice starts to wail, and jumps up onto his lap and hugs him around the neck as she buries her face into his shoulder. I just scoot back along the carpet and sit at his feet, with my hand firmly holding his pants leg.

5.

For the next few days, life was strange. Lee Harvey Oswald, the man who shot Kennedy, was killed as he was being walked to a police car in a parking garage. It was caught on film, and every TV news station played it over and over. The president's funeral was held, and my parents watched it live on television. I finally got to go outside and play with my friends, and there was no school on Monday!

I was too young to understand terms like the loss of innocence. But I could sense the changes in the adults in my life. My father was sad for a long time after that November day. He rarely talked about politics or world affairs. He would watch the news of the Vietnam war beaming into our living room and sigh, his frustration mounting. There didn't seem to be much good news on television until the excitement of the space race replaced Vietnam body counts. We could all take pride in launching men into space, and it helped us escape the worldly realities of war, racism and violence.

6.

It was about twelve years after Kennedy's assassination that I saw my tall, strong, red-headed father cry again. This time, he had leukemia and was close to the end. He cried as he held my hand, apologizing for his weakened condition.

At my father's wake, I slipped a small picture of President Kennedy into his casket. I leaned it on his pants leg.

I DRINKS A BIT

My first drink is a fuzzy combination of myth and memory. My family claims that I got beer in my baby bottle.

I don't recall.

The legend goes something like this:

My Dad and Uncle Fred were taking care of me. I was restless and crying. They put a few ounces of Guinness Stout, topped with Budweiser in a small bottle.

They stuck the nipple in my mouth and carried me off to a crib.

I drank, passed out, and pissed the bed.

Not unlike my adult drinking behavior.

TALL TALES

Over the years, my father gave me some wonderful advice.

Three points, in particular, stand above the rest. He shared his amazing intellect and practical experience in great measure, but these nuggets have stayed with me, and I remember them every single day.

1. He advised me to be a gentleman at all costs.

2. Dad also warned me about drinking beer directly from a bottle. He liked his beer as much as the next guy and he always poured it into a glass.

3. And, father stressed the importance of words on paper. He told me that, to avoid a lifetime of working with my back, if I'd learn the secret of placing words, in the correct order, on paper, I'd make my living with my head, not my hands. (In retrospect, it has been a wash. I've done everything from driving a semi- truck, to arduous military service and writing and producing documentary films.)

An appreciation for words, and the stories they tell, runs deep through my father's ancestry. His people were from Ireland, and before that, Scotland. In his usual self deprecating way, he told me our family was from a long line of people that were such garrulous nonconformists, that we were politely asked to leave not one, but two of

Her Majesty's Sovereign States. As a result of this, I've suffered a bit of an identity crisis.

As a boy, I lived in a blue-collar, Roman Catholic parish, made up of many first and second-generation Irish immigrant families. As a "Mick" I just assumed we were Irish.

Then, in my late forties, my mother revealed to me that my paternal great-grandfather was Scottish.

Great Grand Dad was born in the small town of Kirkcudbright, in Dumfries and Galloway, on the River Dee. There is a family castle there, and befittingly, it was lost in several bad business deals and sits now a ruined hulk without a roof. With my new found knowledge and enthusiasm of my recent Scottishness, I immediately turned to Google, and by the end of the week I'd ordered a Clan MacLellan kilt!

There is something about being more Scottish, and less Shanty Irish, that appeals to me. And, from what I've been told by my wife's kind female friends, I cut a dashing figure in my formal tartan kilt and waist jacket. Ah yes, the clothes make the man!

So, I am tasked by kith and kin with an obligation to tell stories. Blame it on my DNA, or my Attention Deficit Disorder. Either way, I've come to appreciate this ancestral gift, and have loquaciously practiced it for decades. And there is that "words on paper" thing stressed by my dad. If he were still with us, he'd have worn out his Kindle by now.

Twenty-four years out from my last bottle of beer, I claim no gentlemanly drinking custom. I got the booze into my system as efficiently as possible, and pouring it into a glass was just another needless step between me and a good load. Maybe dad insisted on partaking from a nice glass because it forced him to slow down and enjoy his drink.

I drank to get drunk.

There was little enjoyment in the process.

For all one knows this is also a peculiarity conferred on me by my forebears.

I can only remember seeing my father drunk one time, and I'm pretty sure he must have had a good reason. He was drinking brandy at our next-door neighbor's kitchen table and a few hours later had to be helped across the porch and up the stairs to bed.

I'm sure he was using a glass.

Maybe a really big one.

JACK

My clothes smelled like gasoline.

The crisp, white Hess station work uniform was no match for the grime of an all night shift running a small gas station on Rising Sun Avenue. Hess was proud of their bright, clean, green and white stations, with sparkling bathrooms and smiling twenty-four hour pump attendants.

I was just happy to have a decent summer job.

Arriving at eleven p.m. and working until just after daylight, this was my first self directed opportunity. No supervisors or coworkers were around to spoil my shift, and as long as I scrubbed the hell out of the place, and settled my cash drawer each morning, the owners were satisfied. It was busy from the time I arrived, until just after two in the morning. That's when the bars closed.

Afterwards, the night was mine.

I learned where the oil dipstick was on just about every car in America. I also became a hell of a multi-tasker, sometimes filling four cars at a time. But the job, in and of itself, was not very intellectually stimulating. The most challenging aspect of the job was adjusting to an overnight schedule. Surely this is where I became a life-long night creature.

After working this humid July night, I came home and used the back door to enter our house. The door opened into the basement, and I stripped out of my oily, smelly uniform, stuffed it into the washing machine with a dash of Clorox bleach, and slipped up to my bedroom in my shorts. I heard my mom in the kitchen, and wished her a good morning. She was getting ready to go visit my dad in the hospital.

He'd been pretty sick after discovering he had leukemia, and was in and out of the hospital all summer. He'd go through some treatments, blood transfusions, and chemo, and be home for a few months.

This was the new normal routine around my house.

I hit the shower. After washing the fumes from my body, I dove into the clean sheets of my bed, and went to sleep.

Then…

Bolting upright, drenched in sweat, my heart was pounding.

There was a faint, high-pitched sound ringing in my head. It had an internal origin. There was no ambient sound in the room at all. The whirling fan blades were frozen in place, and the wind in the trees outside was still. I could not hear anything and for a few anxious seconds, was afraid that I'd somehow gone deaf! There was always street noise, especially in the morning. Normally I can hear the trains beyond Front Street and trucks coming and going from the giant plant around the corner.

It seemed like the room was in a vacuum.

Nothing was moving or making a sound.

Who turned off the fan?

The second hand on my alarm clock had stopped.

Maybe there was a power outage? No, the clock was a wind up type.

It was hard to catch my breath. The air was sucked from the room. The sound was still present, but now the pitch was wavering from high to low.

Suddenly, the whitest, purest light I had ever seen was blazing in from the window.

As bright as it was, it did not blind my eyes. I did not have to look away. It was a healing, friendly light, that gave off overwhelmingly positive energy. The light began to take form. It became like a thousand little slivers of glass circling in the center of the room. The vortex of light became tighter and the glass shards spun faster and faster, forming a floor-to-ceiling mirror.

The room became cold. My breathing stopped and my heart was no longer beating. I didn't need my eyes to see. I was just present, no longer physical. The mirrored light became a million little colors, each one a slightly different hue, never touching one of the same shade. They were alive, with a vivid life force of their own.

Then in a flash, the essence took form.

My Father.

His body was shiny, like it had been dipped in silver. His face was clear and beautiful. His wavy hair was gone, and his head was smooth. His piercing eyes held all the knowledge of his lifetime. My father was in a semi-physical form, fluctuating from matter to energy.

I was not afraid, but in complete awe of the marvelous event that was before me. I brought my hands in front of me, but I could not focus enough to see any detail. I was blurry, without clear definition. Trying to speak, to cry out. I was mute.

Then.

"Robert."

I heard my dad's voice, as clear as ever, entering directly into my consciousness, my soul.

"Robert, it is time for me to leave now son."

"You are a beautiful boy Robert and I love you."

"At all costs, lad, behave like a gentleman."

Everything went black.

The room spun and I was crying out, "Dad! Wait... Dad!"

Then the fan whirred in the window, the wind swept through the trees, and the clock began ticking. It read 9:30.

Rushing downstairs, I called out, "Mom, mom, where are you?"

No one answered. I ran down the basement and looked out into the driveway. Her car was gone.

I sat on the old green sofa in the basement and cried. He was gone. I knew it. It wasn't a bad dream, it really happened. My dad came to say farewell before he went over. I sat there for a long time. Silent.

The phone rang. I ran up to the kitchen to answer it.

"Hello?"

"Bobby," it was my mother, "your father passed away this morning."

"I know."

I hung up.

The week after Dad's funeral my mother gathered my clothes in garbage bags, and dumped all my belongings on the front lawn. She evicted me from our family home, as thoughtlessly as she would put out the trash. I never returned.

A GOOD BAR STOOL

A modest green and white sign is painted over the block glass window:

"ERIN CAFE."

It is not much to look at. A single, narrow storefront near the main shopping avenue in a rough, row home neighborhood, it displays just enough external seediness to keep the meek and curious from entering.

Along the entire wall to the left is an intricately carved chestnut back bar, a testament to the woodworking skills of the immigrants who settled this predominately Catholic Parish. The shelves are not stocked with fine whiskeys and exotic liquors that befit such a work of finely crafted art, but rather, the buck-a-shot Canadian and Kentucky blends of the blue-collar class. You might find some off brand scotch, and, of course - Jamesons.

Bushmills is for Protestants.

There are all the usual American beers on tap and a single import in warm, dark brown bottles: Guinness Stout. No Heineken, St. Pauli Girl or Fosters to be found. And there is absolutely no Bass or Newcastle. In here, to ask about English beers will get you more than a few stern stares, and perhaps a bloody lip.

The jukebox holds a combination of traditional Celtic tunes and contemporary rock music.

This may be the only bar in Philadelphia without a Frank Sinatra song.

A long, polished shuffleboard table runs along the wall at the rear of the room. The quoits sharply clack as they hit each other, and raise a small cloud of sawdust as they tumble from the board's edge.

Lively, animated conversations, most in a lilting Irish American brogue, take place from one end of the bar to the other. The talk orbits loosely around politics, sports and the never ending exploitation of the working class. The language is impassioned and intelligent. This is how the English language was intended to be spoken. Behind the cash register, tacked above a framed portrait of John F. Kennedy, is a printed parchment:

"Profanity is the Attempt of a Feeble Mind to Express Itself."

This is where, (before I was legally able to consume alcohol in Pennsylvania,) I learned to sit a good bar stool.

In the fortunate company of men with strong hands, stout hearts, and nimble minds, I commenced to drink like a poet.

The tavern was run by a handsome Irishman, a former welterweight boxer named Brendan. In his fifties, he was still as solid as his professional ring days, and few men tested him. Brendan was, with his wavy dark hair, twinkling eyes and charming demeanor, a sort of matinee idol. Quick to smile, diplomatic to a fault, and smart as a scholar, he was the Renaissance man of the neighborhood. There was, however, a twenty-year old Interpol warrant issued for him, as he was once tested by a Royal Ulster Constable in a Belfast alley. Brendan was not his real name, and some say his youthful good looks were, in part, a credit to a California plastic surgeon. He didn't carry the mug of a former prize fighter. He worked the gold mines of the Yukon, the oil fields of Alaska, and every pretty girl he ever met. He claimed to be my father's distant cousin, so I respectfully called him "Uncle" in public.

As much as Brendan was the gregarious front man, the silent Micky McHugh was the Erin's unassuming owner. He opened the doors at six-thirty every morning, and settled the cash register after closing at 2 a.m. Mary Kate, his dedicated wife, tended bar in the daytime. Kate was a big-boned, larger than life, six foot-two inches tall. Her upswept red hair made her appear as a freckled Gaelic Amazon. They rarely acknowledged the other's presence, yet seemed to be telepathically connected. No one can recall them ever uttering a cross word to anyone. Francis X. McGinley, the bishop at St. Helen church, was Mary Kate's brother and one of Micky's best friends. Mary Kate was as wide awake as anyone could be, and nothing that took place in the Erin escaped her notice. They were as respected a married couple as one could hope to emulate. Yet, Micky's permanently furrowed brow, divulged the silent, stormy sea brewing deep within.

One Wednesday evening in May, Micky invited me and Seamus O'Brien to join him at the little front corner table that served as his office. Paper invoices and order sheets were neatly piled in tight little stacks in front of him.

"Brendan, send a few beers over for the lads, please," he said as he motioned for us to sit opposite him.

As we were settling down, Brendan arrived with a couple of cold Rolling Rocks for Obie and me, and a tall ginger ale for Micky. As he spun to leave, the former champ punched me sharply on the arm, leaned in close and said,

"Listen attentively lad, and make me proud to be yer uncle."

Micky began.

"Brendan thinks highly of you two. He tells me you know your way around New York and Jersey already. He says you are mature young men."

"Yes, thanks Mr. McHugh", I said looking Obie in the eye.

"We like New York. We were there last month for an Alice Cooper concert."

Seamus chimed in, "I don't think Mr. McHugh knows who Alice Cooper is, Bobby. And probably doesn't care, either."

"Well lads, you may be surprised by what I know. His songs are on me jukebox; they get played a good bit, you see." McHugh proudly stated. "I know where every nickel is spent in this tavern."

"Sorry sir," Obie offered meekly.

"Nothing to apologize about Seamus, just be a lesson learned."

McHugh clinked his glass against Obie's green beer bottle.

"Now, boys. As much as we all like him, we didn't sit down to discuss the finer points of Mr. Cooper's music."

Obie and I laughed nervously and shifted forward in our chairs.

"Would you gentlemen enjoy a train ride to New York this week? And an easy three hundred dollars to ride that train?"

My eyes widened.

"Sure, yes we would, wouldn't we Obie?"

Seamus nodded.

"Okay then."

Micky handed me a manila envelope taken from under one of his paper stacks. "You take these two tickets, ride the AmTrak from 30th street to Penn Station, put something in a locker for me, come back, and report to Brendan."

I started to open the envelope.

"No! Do not open it until you are at 30th street station," he snapped.

"You will find two keys in there as well."

I jiggled the envelope and felt the keys.

"Seamus, you will take the blue key and open the locker it belongs to at 30th street. In the locker is a little leather briefcase. Put the briefcase in a back pack, or some sort of duffle bag - you don't look like the executive type," he continued.

"In New York, Bobby, you take the briefcase out of the duffle and place it in the locker at Penn Station."
"There is a white key that fits the locker."

"How do we know where to find the lockers?" I asked almost whispering.

"Brendan says you boys are bright," He asks sarcastically "Should I be doubting my life long friend?"

"No sir, no problem, we'll figure it out," I offer confidently.

"Of course you will, lad. All the details are inside the envelope."

"Now Bobby you are the crew leader on this, so I expect you to live up to expectations." McHugh says.

"Your train leaves 30th Street Station at 2:30 tomorrow afternoon."

"Thank you Mr. McHugh," I say.

"Yeah, thanks," Obie offers.

In an instant, Brendan swoops over picks up our half finished beers.

Handing us each 15 crisp twenty-dollar bills, he orders "Don't come back in here until the trip is over."

He warns, "And don't come back here at all if anything goes wrong, got that lads?"

"Geez, Uncle Brendan, nothing is going to go wrong," I volunteer.

"I almost feel guilty taking Micky's money."

"Well don't son. And lads, there is nothing in that case you need to know about."

"And it's not any dope or drugs, so don't be paranoid. Just some business that needs to be done with discretion."

His eyes twinkle as he sees us to the door.

"And discretion, me laddies, is the better part of valor!"

The next day we took the Frankford El down to 30th Street. It was a pretty quiet ride. Obie brought this bright orange duffle thing, some Coast Guard surplus bag, I think.

"Holy Shit Ob," I teased him, "Why don't you just paint a big 'Hey cops, please fuck with us' sign to carry up to New York?"

"We ain't doin' nothing wrong" he countered, "just taking a package somewhere for your uncle...and that ain't against the law."

"Come 'on Ob, you know this isn't completely innocent," I whispered.

"Otherwise, why get two assholes like us to do it?"

I leaned closer and whispered even softer, "If it was legit, they'd just drive up and deliver it themselves."

"Hey man," Obie says firmly, "I don't EVEN want to know what it is."

"But you got some ideas, right" I say.

"Like you don't?" Obie answers.

Obie continues, "You know the political shit Micky's into-and Brendan ain't exactly who everybody thinks he is now is he?"

"I'm not so sure I'd pretend he was my uncle, if I was you," he advises.

"Well he's cooler than any of my real uncles," I say, "and I ain't asking questions or saying shit to him about anything!"

I continue, "Let's just go to New York and come home and spend three hundred bucks on a good party."

Despite our pounding hearts and sweaty palms we pulled it off without a hitch.

When we turned the keys over to Brendan, he generously gave us each an additional hundred dollars and an unexpected kiss on the cheek.

Suddenly, Mary Kate took us both by the arm and out the back door to the narrow alley. She held each of our hands in hers and offered some cryptic advice: "You're in it now lads-no longer standing by."

"But you can make other plans, you're young and bright enough to choose your battles and not inherit the fate."

"I love you both enough to tell you, the next time you accept a task from old Provos like Brendan and Micky, your choice will be made for you."

She whacked us on our rear ends and said,"Besides, you lads are too young to be drinking in me pub!"

"Next time I see ya in 'ere, I'm cardin' and flaggin' ya both!"

More than thirty years have passed and I've never had another drink in the Erin.

PAPAL PARADE

It is a big day in Philadelphia.

The Pope is coming.

Sitting in Dirty Franks bar, on Pine street, I am drinking cold Rolling Rocks and watching the local news anchors cover the motorcade as it winds its way through South Philly up Broad Street. I am on a rickety old barstool, only a block away from the main route.

The TV screens in the bar show throngs of enthusiastic people lining the streets blessing themselves with the sign of the cross while Pope John Paul smiles and waves to his faithful flock.

As the newscasters announce that the motorcade is approaching Catherine Street, a handful of us decide to run over to Broad and Pine to witness history, the Pontiff's holy visit.

There are thousands of people, three or four deep, on the sidewalk here in the center of this largely catholic city. I elbow my way to a front-row position and press against the wooden police barrier that separates us from the great infallible spiritual leader.

As his vehicle slowly drives by, I raise my fresh green pony bottle in a symbolic toast to His Holiness.

It is over quickly and I jog back to Franks, reclaiming my seat and ordering another beer.

Unknown to me at the time, it will not be the last time I see Pope John Paul in person.

I am such a fallen catholic.

Thank Christ.

HEY BO!

The box office is closed.

The blinds have been drawn tightly shut and a "Sold Out" sign taped to the glass.

It is a raw January evening, and the little space heater under the counter has turned this place into a miniature sauna. The young girl who sells tickets and answers the phone takes call after call, replying the same way each time.

"I'm sorry the Bo Diddley show is sold out."

"I'm sorry, tonight's show is sold out."

I'm in this tight space with her, looking for a booking agent's phone number in the Rolodex. There are no tickets left. And, just two hours before showtime, there is no act either. I'm getting nervous.

I find the number and grab the phone from her. We both get wrapped up in the long cord in this cramped space that was intended only for one person at a time.

Tap!

Tap! Tap!

On the glass.

I reach around the girl and dial the phone.

Rap!

Rap! Rap!

On the glass.

The young girl lets out a heavy sigh as she peeks through the blinds to see who is banging on her window with a heavy ring.

"Bo Diddley."

The girl shouts the now familiar refrain through the glass.

"I'm sorry the Bo Diddley show is sold out."

She plops back down onto her stool.

The agent's phone is ringing and ringing. Finally, it transfers me to a voice mail. I frantically alert him that I've got a sold out club and his act is late. I'm really beginning to worry.

Bang!

Bang! Bang!

On the glass.

The exasperated girl jerks the blinds open.

"I TOLD YOU!" she yells.

"The Bo Diddley show is sold out!"

With a red face, she slams the blinds closed.

"I swear, some people!"

Bam!

"I"

Bam!

"AM"

Bam!

"BO"

Bam!

"DIDDLEY!"

Bam! Bam! Bam!

I almost knock the girl over as I run from the box office to unlock the front door.

"I'm so sorry!", I say.

He sweeps past me with his dark collar turned up and a long purple scarf wrapped around his neck. In his familiar bowler hat and large framed eyeglasses, he is an unmistakeable American musical icon. I take his guitar case and shoulder bag from him and continue to apologize profusely.

"Where's that little girl," he asks.

Oh crap. He's going to rip her a new one for making him stand outside in the cold.

He makes a bee line for the box office.

The embarrassed girl sheepishly comes out and meets him.

Taking her little hand in his, he leans down close to her ear.

"Don't you worry, been happenin' for thirty years up here in these white clubs, sweetheart."

He turns to me.

"I've paid my dues enough to walk through the front door."

Indeed, Bo Diddley!

REPO

The little blue Subaru is the first new car I've ever owned. I am four payments behind. The finance company has been trying to contact me, but I let the answering machine pick up all my calls these days.

They are not the only bill collectors I'm avoiding.

There are big guys in expensive suits from South Philly who are first in line.

I've pretty much stopped working a legitimate job. My addiction has run off any future prospects of stage management gigs. I am a ticking time bomb in a business where reliability means everything.

My sanity is also in question.

It has gotten to the point where I don't care.

On the few production gigs I can scrape up, I don't give a shit at what end of the room the stage is located. I just want to get high and sell cocaine to the acts and their crews.

I know it is low rent and it makes me feel like a failure.

My alienated friends, coworkers and acquaintances have deserted me. I'm picking up bar band mixing gigs instead of professional clubs and arena shows.

Who cares?

Just as many coke heads in a bar as backstage at a big show. Besides, my reputation actually means something at this level.

"I've worked with everyone from U2 to Ray Charles," I crow to the lonely waitresses. These are the only ones who still listen. For their attention, they are rewarded with endless lines of rock star quality coke.

My life sucks and the only thing keeping me from ending it is my fucking ego.

I am afraid of living like this, but more fearful of the mess I'd leave behind. I don't want to be remembered as this person in the mirror today.

I owe about twelve-hundred bucks on the Subaru. Even though I have almost five thousand dollars on the razor blade scarred mirror in front of me, I hide out, watching from the bedroom window as the tow truck pulls it away.

I do a huge line and phone for a taxi.

I am such a pussy.

THE STEPS

The concrete steps lead up to a row house on the corner of Torresdale Avenue and Levick Street. There is a camera shop at street level and these steep steps run along the skinny path between the tiny store and the space above.

At street level there is a little board with meeting times posted. On each step is a hand printed saying of some kind. I am not sure what they mean. What kind of meeting is held here? It is no doubt some religious organization because the term "GOD" and "HIGHER POWER" appear in some of the painted passages. They are obviously lifted from a section of the Bible with which I am not familiar.

Over a Philly cheese steak at a luncheonette across the street, my Uncle Eddie suggested I check out the meetings at this place. Ed used to be the most notorious drunk in our extended family. He miraculously cleaned up, found a good woman, and has stayed sober for a few years now.

Eddie is my mother's brother and is divorced from my father's sister. He is my closest older male relative. I tell him he's my uncle. "squared." He doesn't get it and thinks I'm accusing him of being "uncool."

He works the graveyard shift at the tractor parts plant around the corner from my apartment. Once in a while we share a quick bite at Gloria's Deli.

I am twenty years old, with a good job, a cool girlfriend, and I usually have a few a dollars in my pocket. Life should be good.

But I am miserable.

You would never know it from meeting me, but I am torn up inside.

I am tired, scared, and not sure about anything in my life. I drink every night until I pass out. It is the only way I can quiet the noise in my head. It is a cacophony of voices - my own disturbed conscience. I question my sanity on a daily basis. I feel dark and dirty inside.

Eddie has been around a few times when I've expressed some anxiety. He talks to me about things that matter. My ideas, dreams, and plans for life. He is encouraging, and is the only person in my family that is remotely optimistic. My father died three years ago, and Eddie sat by him in the hospital every night. After we buried dad, Eddie went away. Rumor is that he went away to a treatment center for alcoholics. My mother said he went to the nuthouse. It doesn't matter to me. He doesn't talk much about his experience, just says that he is happy living his life today, not just enduring it. I want some of what Uncle Ed has. But I am not going to a nut-house to get it.

There are some guys on the porch of the mystery steps house. They just got off motorcycles and are wearing leather cuts. Maybe this is a Biker for Jesus cult thing? I swallow hard and start up the steps. I read a little from each one. Oh boy, this is strange.

Approaching the porch, one of the guys turns and sticks out his tattooed hand. "My name's Carl…welcome."

I stutter, "mm…m…my name's Robert…"

"First time here?" asks another big biker guy.

"Ahhh…yep." I mutter.

"Just listen, take what you can use, and leave the rest," offers Carl.

"There's coffee on inside."

I timidly open the door and step inside.

My eyes adjust and I make out a big wooden conference table surrounded by folding chairs. There are those sayings again, this time numbered from one through twelve and on a giant wall poster. I don't fail to notice the capitalized spelling of G-O-D and P-O-W-E-R.

There are a few men standing around in the kitchen watching a big stainless coffee pot.

Again, the introductions; "My names Roy...Call me Tiny...I'm Danny..."

"Welcome"

"Welcome"

"Keep coming back..."

The coffee is ready and someone hands me a Styrofoam cup.

"Black?"...

"Sure," I whisper.

He pours for me. What the hell is this place? These guys are hard knock dudes, not the Jesus freak type. My kind of guys. Tough men from the streets. But they have a soft demeanor. Some of the guys are familiar faces from the neighborhood.

The room fills quickly and I am offered a seat at the table. Instead, I sit in a chair along the wall. There is some reading from a prepared text and after the leaders read they all recite some prayer together.

The Big Book.

The Steps.

The Traditions.

I am at meeting of Alcoholics Anonymous!

But I thought alcoholics were all homeless bums who dived in dumpsters and lived in camps under bridges...!

The men introduce themselves as alcoholics and drug addicts, and then proceed to say a little something to the group about their lives. Some are horror stories of drugs and drinking. Others are just the usual dumb assed things that they are having a hard time with…jobs…wives…bills.

I am sure I am in the wrong place, but I don't have the courage to get up and leave. Besides, some of these cats are hard asses from the corners and may not like me leaving early. I don't want to appear disrespectful.

I sit and sweat. I also have to piss but am too scared to ask for the bathroom.

Trying to keep my shit together, I am suddenly struck with a fear I have never known. The guy running the meeting has pointed to me and asks if I'd like to say anything. If I'd like to share my thoughts.

My heart races and I am paralyzed.

I stammer and cough and say. "No, not today…" like I was fending off a pop quiz from my second grade teacher.

They all stand, and so I do. There is a circle of hand holding guys forming and I am the only one who does not join the ring. They say the Lord's Prayer and a chant while holding hands. Then there is much backslapping and joviality. Some of them hug everyone in sight.

I can't get out of this place fast enough, but my progress is hindered by big guys who are shaking my hand, slapping my shoulders and asking me a million questions:

"Have you been sober long?"

NO!

"Do you have a sponsor?"

NO!

"What other meetings do you go to?"

NONE!

Want to go get some coffee across the street?"

NO!

I am trapped.

I'm pretty sure there is going to be a baptism or circumcision.

I am the guest of honor.

I have to get out of here!

I am sweating and hyperventilating and all this talk of drugs and drinking makes me want to get very fucked up.

Fast.

I don't need this A.A. noise bouncing around in my head.

I'm almost to the door and Carl corners me. He hands me a long piece of paper.

"If you feel like drinking or drugging, call one of these numbers first and someone will come get you to a meeting…"

Practically running down the steps I am met by Tiny.

He waits at the bottom. As I try to pass, he reaches for my hand.

"I remember my first meeting, " he says.

He puts a huge hand around my bicep.

"You'll never forget what you found here tonight, and it is going to fuck up your drinking big time."

Tiny punched me in the arm, nodded, and straddled his Harley.

I walked a few blocks away and straddled a stool at the Horseshoe bar.

Thirteen years later, I came back to Alcoholics Anonymous.

And kept coming back.

SO YOU WANNA BE
A ROCK AND ROLL STAR?

Most of the band is on stage and sound check may be a reality soon.

Then all Hell breaks loose.

Ms. Rock Star refuses to come down from the dressing rooms. She is not pleased with the backstage hospitality. Not unusual. She's another eccentric rock goddess with an attitude problem.

We are already behind schedule, and I go up to defuse the situation.

Opening the door to the dressing room, I see the punked-out diva tossing a fit and yelling at her overwhelmed manager. They are surrounded by the usual cast of backstage flunkies: record label reps, a stylist, publicists, a few music journalists, hangers-on and radio DeeJays. She is putting on quite a show for her posse.

I walk over, introduce myself and ask what I can do to sort things out and get her down to the stage.

She gets right up in my face and says, "You can get me the six fucking bottles of Pepsi, just like it says in my rider! This cheap fountain soda bullshit is Coke, and I don't fucking drink Coke!"

I have seen backstage tantrums before, and may have even caused a few, but this carrying on over cola was a new one for me. We're a small music club and most acts are just happy with our best effort to provide meals and refreshments. Besides, it is usually the hangers-on and crew that wind up eating and drinking everything in the dressing rooms.

Quick assessment: This chick's nuts.

I try to calm her down and say, "Okay, I'll send someone out for the Pepsi, but right now we need you downstairs for sound check. By the time you are finished, we'll have it up here waiting for you."

Just then, Mr. Manager Man steps between us, pokes me in the chest with his skinny finger and says, "She doesn't leave this room until she has Pepsi."

I grab his wrist, twisting his arm up behind his back, and he goes down on one knee. He is in shock.

"Don't touch me you skinny fuck," I say, "You poke me again, I'll break your frickin' arm and beat you with it!"

His mouth opens but he can't seem to speak.

The roomful of useful idiots turns to instant chaos. Some run for the door, others are jumping on the furniture and screaming.

Ms. Rock Star throws a full pitcher of the offending cola on me and screams, "Here's your fucking Coca-Cola, asshole!"

I sure did a good job of "defusing the situation..."

By now, some of my crew have heard the ruckus and rush up to the dressing rooms. I've got sticky cola all over my face, in my hair, and running down the front of me. I move towards the door to help Brad, my sound guy, get through the throng in the small space. Mr. Manager is still holding his injured arm, rubbing it with tears in his eyes shouting something about lawsuits and lawyers.

Ms. Rock Star is screaming for security. I grab her by her black leather vest and say, "Get these fucking people out of here before someone else gets hurt." Surprisingly, she softens a bit, maybe realizing her absurd farce has gone too far and quietly says, "Okay, no problem."

She steps aside, wheels back around, balls up her fist, and punches me like a middleweight boxer - right on the jaw!

Things get fuzzy.

I stumble and fall to the sofa.

Holy shit! She cold-cocked me like a man!

Bradley grabs her in a bear hug and lifts all hundred-ten pounds of squirming, screaming banshee off the ground. Her feet are not touching the floor.

Just then, Big Lou, the former NFL lineman who provides our front-of-house security, crashes into the room.

He surveys the mess and says, "What the hell?"

He puts a huge hand on Bradley's neck, squeezes it and says, "Put her down, Brad."

Lou takes the screaming, spitting woman by the arm and gently guides her through the inner door to the restroom.

After a few moments, Lou emerges. He grabs me from the sofa by my wet, stinking shirt and says in a stage whisper, "Get in there and apologize - Oh, and she told me you've got balls - she likes you."

The show was a sell out. Ms. Rock Star looked and sounded great.

The single from her debut album topped the charts all summer.

IN THE NAVY

My Senior Chief called me into his office.

"Hey Mack, you think you look good in green?"

"Um...okay Senior, I guess so," I stammered.

"Good, 'cause there's a Seabee battalion on the west coast that needs a combat photographer."

"But, well, I'm not trained as a combat photographer, I haven't had that advanced tech sch..."

"No shit, Sherlock. You start Combat Camera school next Tuesday. I've already got your seat," he offered. "Do you want these orders or not, Mack?"

"What about my other orders to the Eisenhower?"

"Fuck the Ike. There are plenty of photo turds that would love to go to that aircraft carrier," he said, "I recommended you to the 'Bees 'cause I think you can handle independent duty - you think on your feet."

I was sweating. I hated moments like this, but my life seemed full of them. Too many good choices. Option "A" seemed good, but maybe option "B" would be better? It was a curse.

After previously learning I was going to the U.S.S. Eisenhower, I researched everything I could get my hands on about that ship. CVN-69, one of the nuclear powered super carriers, was a floating city. The prospect of sailing the world, seeing exotic ports, working with state-of-the-art camera systems and aircraft, seemed pretty exciting. I didn't know anything about the Seabees except they were almost the Marine Corps and John Wayne did a movie about them. They were such a small, specialized part of the Navy, that I didn't even know they had photographers on board. And the 'Bees had a rough image.

So much for skating through a stint in the Navy.

If I wanted to be in Special Forces, I'd have joined the Army.

LUQUILLO BEACH

Part One

The dusty parking lot has large mosquito-infested puddles of stagnant water, tourist vomit and piss. Around the perimeter are dozens of crowded kioskos; small crudely built beer and fried fish stands. Each one is numbered and painted in whatever color was on sale that week. I am attempting to drink at least one beer from each little shack this weekend. I'm an ambitious, goal-oriented drunk. At beer number eleven, it is too damn hot out here, and the flies are getting annoying as they compete for the battered squid that I am shoveling into my mouth as fast as I can. It gives me stinky fingers.

Wrangling my partner Randall from the surf, I convince him that we need to go inside the pink hotel across the road, and drink at the air conditioned bar. He's been body surfing while wearing an embarrassingly tight yellow swim brief. He's a dark, hairy guy, and the suit doesn't contribute to his usual Mormon modesty. The beach is full of locals attending a big music festival, and his tiny see-through Speedo elicits a few awkward stares. I guess he doesn't know any better.

Randall's a reliable partner, who drinks like a normal person, keeping me out of trouble on these off-base ventures into the surrounding Puerto Rican culture.

Covering himself in a jogging suit (also yellow!) Randy catches up with me as I open the big glass doors.

"Hey Mac, did you see the topless chicks laying out?" he asks like a man who has never seen a bare breast before.

"Most of those girls are here with their families, Randall, and they are not going to let two gringo sailors get anywhere near them!" I reply, seeking the promising coolness of the Luquillo Beachside Taberna, just off the main lobby.

Stepping down into the bar, I hear Bob Seger tunes from the jukebox. Things are looking up. This is a much more comfortable drinking arrangement than the steamy mess across the dusty road. My eyes adjust quickly to the neon oasis.

"Por favor, dos Heinekens." I slap a twenty on the solid wooden bar and we slip onto heavy padded barstools.

Venezuelan baseball is on a big screen at the end of the bar. There are about ten people, mostly couples, in the place, and Randy and I are the only customers speaking English. The beers are ice cold and the AC is pumping. Heineken number twelve was the best of the day.

"What's with the yellow outfit?" I ask Randy in a very accusatory tone.

"It was on sale at the Navy Exchange," he offers sheepishly.

"I know why," I say.

"Hey man," Randall snaps a bit agitated, "I've got child support for six kids in California, I can't be a fashion plate."

"I'm going to buy you a decent pair of straight men's swim trunks before you get on that beach again," I laugh.

"What's wrong with my bathing suit, Mac?" he asks.

"Well, my best buddy, don't take this wrong, but you look as gay as can be in those canary panties."

"Fuck you!' he snaps, "buy us another beer, before I kiss you in public and ruin your chances with the local girls."

Part Two: LOCAL GIRLS

At beer number thirteen, two dark haired, mocha-skinned women wander into the bar from the side door. They are speaking Spanish, laughing, and don't seem to notice the rest of the world as they continue their animated conversation, barely pausing for a breath.

The girls hop up to the bar almost opposite us. The older one makes eye contact and I smile. She holds my glance for just a fraction of a second longer than a casual glimpse. Her friend continues to talk in a giggly staccato.

Beer number fourteen arrives and Randall and I are singing along to the jukebox. The other patrons seem amused, politely tolerant of our off-key harmonies.

I wander over to the jukebox, and as I am studiously rolling through the selections, the woman I smiled at walks up beside me.

"Do you need help picking the songs?", she asks, in accented English keeping her eyes down and studying the titles. About half of them are in Spanish.

I am startled at first. She is at least a foot shorter than me and the warm red and orange light makes her skin look like caramel. She looks up, smiles warmly, and says approvingly "You sing in public, most Americans are too self-conscious."

"I'm certainly not shy, and I've had enough beers already to not care," I laugh. "I try to sing the wrong notes with the right feeling."

"I like men who sing," she says as she punches in some numbers to the jukebox.

As quickly as she appeared, she slipped away and rejoined her friend.

I finished selecting songs and made my way back to the bar.

"Wow, Mac, what is it about you that women want to talk to you?" Randall asks.

"It is a curse," I say as I ignore him and attempt to make eye contact with the woman.

"You don't want to catch it."

The scratchy speakers blast out a Tom Petty song and Randy and I resume our off-key singing when the chorus rolls around.

The girls stop their conversation and look at us.

The older one, again smiles and starts to sing along softly. The younger, giggly girl laughs and tries to join in, but apparently doesn't speak English well enough to know the lyrics.

The song finishes and we all laugh spontaneously. Randy is instantly up out of his seat and over at their side of the bar.

A little too enthusiastic, as usual.

If he gets lucky, this will be exactly the second woman Randall has had sex with in his young life. His wife, whom he began dating at fifteen, recently ran off with their family doctor.

The girls shake his hand and the older one replies, "Mucho gusto, I am Carolina and this is my niece, Dolly."

I get up and, instead of joining them, I head to the men's room, taking the long way around and through the lobby.

One of the Spanish songs Carolina picked is now playing.

"Randy is such a loser," I whisper into the bathroom mirror, as I check my teeth and splash cool water over my face. "Carolina, eh? Little caramel-colored Carolina."

Part Three: CAROLINA

It is eight in the evening and the sun is just beginning to set behind the verdant green hills beyond the stage. The four of us have eaten a nice meal at the beach hotel and gotten to know one another a little better. I stopped drinking after beer number fifteen. I switched to cold tea and may even be sobering up a little.

All very casual, and the two girls gave us no opportunity to romance them. They insisted on paying their own checks. They have a room at the hotel, and went up to change clothes, promising to meet us at the music festival. They did not invite us up.

Randy and I share an appreciation of all styles of music, so a big Puerto Rican music festival with two local women as company, is a heck of a good way to spend the evening.

"I don't see them anywhere, Mac," Randy nervously scans the crowd, which has swelled to a few thousand people as the show begins.

"Relax Rand, let them find us," I say confidently. "We are a lot easier to pick out in this local crowd than they are."

Salsa music is blasting, the horns are wailing, and the crowd is undulating like a giant multi-colored tropical organism. This is great!

The announcer is apparently a DJ from the big radio station in San Juan. He brings out the next act, and to my surprise it is Eddie Gomez! Eddie is a bass player from the Bronx, who has played with all the funk-rock greats.

"Wow, Randy, this is Eddie Gomez, from the States," I yell above the din.

"Cool," he replies, "I saw him with Zappa."

Gomez and his band are laying the funk down thick and the audience near the stage is a sweltering dance machine. The temperature must be ninety-five and the atmosphere is feverish.

I figure we have been stood up, but Randall continues to scan behind him, hoping the two girls will show.

"You should give it a break and enjoy the show," I say. "Get into the music and be in the moment."

You're right Mac, but they were very cool chicks," he says dejectedly.

"This place is full of cool chicks Rand, look around you!"

We move closer to the stage after Gomez' set and the emcee is conducting some kind of radio station contest with the winners being called up to receive new Sony Walkmans.

The house band begins playing some pop/rock salsa tune and he announces the next act. It is a woman singer in a colorful traditional dress and the crowd reacts with cheers, screams and whistles. She has already begun singing, but can't be heard because of the noise from the audience, who are singing along with every word.

"Holy shit, Mac!" Randall states the obvious.

"That's the girl from the hotel..that's her...from dinner...wow, that Carolina chick, she's a singer."

I laugh with him saying, "Well at least we didn't get stood up."

Holy crap, Mac, she must be...like...famous."

Part Four: FAMOUS

Carolina is an actress who plays a comedic character on a Spanish language TV soap opera, or "novella." She is heavily made up for the part, looking much older and somewhat frumpy and asexual. She is anything but.

Carolina is also a very popular singer, who, when she was a teenager, had several songs at the top of the Latin American charts.

People recognize her and sometimes ask for an autograph. Especially young girls.

I didn't date her because she was a pop star. I liked her because she was bright, attractive, interesting and down-to-earth. Before joining the Navy, I spent my early twenties doing stage production with some of the biggest names in the music business. Being around famous people was not new to me. I think Carolina appreciates this.

I also appreciate the wild, edgy, multiple partner sex. Carolina is bisexual and I am not complaining. She and I shared the same taste in women.

Plus, we have both escaped really bad marriages.

Part Five: MARRIAGE

Carolina and I have been seeing each other, and getting very hot and heavy for about ten months. I must now return to California with my military unit.

"You can stay here," Carolina offers, gesturing around her beautiful San Juan condo overlooking the sea. "We will get married and you can transfer to the base at Roosevelt Roads."

"It's not that simple," I say. "I'm not up for a transfer for more than a year, and have another deployment to Sicily in a few months."

"If I stay here, I'll be arrested for desertion—and this is U.S. territory."

Don't remind me of that unpleasant fact right now," she growls.

Carolina is active in the political party supporting Puerto Rican independence.

"Let's just enjoy the time we have together, until we can work something out," I offer meekly, stepping closer to hug her.

Carolina cries. It is strange being around such a skilled actress. I never know when her emotions are sincere or when she is conjuring up a part.

Being particularly conscious to never promise anything beyond the present with Carolina, in the course of our time together, I have always been aware that I will leave. This was always a finite journey for me. There has always been a period at the end of my sentence.

I am also an alcoholic, trying desperately to find some sobriety, and Carolina has a drinking problem.

Through several detoxes, treatment centers, AA, NA, and pure willpower, in the course of the last couple of years I've managed to put together a few months of sobriety. I have liked being sober more than being a drunk. When I return to the states I am planning to go back to inpatient treatment and do what it takes to quit for good. There is no way I can stop drinking with Carolina. She lives the cafe life. A dedicated hedonist, she throws herself into the wildest of parties until she passes out, and I have to carry her home. She rarely remembers this.

We have had some serious talks about our co-dependent drinking, but I think Carolina feigns language translation difficulty when I bring it up. If she was willing to attempt sobriety, I'd consider hanging around.

I need to choose between Carolina and sobriety.

Part Six: SOBRIETY

There have been letters and occasional telephone conversations over the past year. Carolina continues to invite me to come and live in Puerto Rico.

I have spent a lot of time in AA meetings. I've found some solace and spiritual understanding while pursuing my Buddhist studies. In the past year I have been sober more often than drunk. I like sober. It is an everyday struggle, and some days I come up short, but I am beginning to see the light.

Checking my box at the Battalion mail room, there is a package from Puerto Rico. Inside is an American Airlines ticket from L.A. to San Juan. There is a smaller envelope and a bright Puerto Rican greeting card depicting folk dancers in traditional dress. Inside is a note and a theater ticket:

My Dearest Robert:

Please come to my island and share my proudest professional achievement. There is no other man with whom I would prefer to spend this special evening.

All my love,

Carolina

Carolina is going to premiere a one-woman show, a tribute to legendary salsa singer, Celia Cruz. The venue is the Belles Artes, Puerto Rico's national theater. The show is sold out for its first ten performances.

The airline ticket is round trip. Okay, I'll go. I can handle this. I've got some time off coming to me and I've been sober almost six weeks.

I may have to buy a new suit. It will have to be tropical.

Part Seven: TROPICAL

My plane is early arriving at Luis Munoz Marin airport in San Juan. I call Carolina from a pay phone and agree to take a taxi to her place. It is only a ten minute ride, anyway.

"You here from Florida?" the taxi driver asks as we cross the long bridge from Isla Verde.

"No, no California, actually," I reply.

The tropical heat has hit me like a brick and my brain is frying in his poorly air conditioned cab.

"Here on business?" the happy cabbie asks.

"No, seeing a friend," I offer as San Juan landmarks pass by in a blurry mirage of heat and casual familiarity.

"Ahhh, a girl," he guesses, "A Puertoricana?"

"Yeah, I met her when I was stationed here a while back."

"A sailor, a Navy man?" he asks.

"Yes sir, a Seabee," now wondering how I got into this conversation in the first place.

In a moment of arrogance or stupidity I add:

"You may know her."

"Really, who is she?" he eagerly says as he sizes me up me in the rear view mirror.

"Carolina Lydia Contador," I answer.

"No!" he says disbelieving. "Carolina Lydia - the singer? The actress?"

"I'm here as her guest...for the opening of her new show," I smugly add.

I can't believe I am doing this. Big deal...I am the former wayward lover of one your cultural treasures. Why do I feel so superior to this nice little guy? It is the latent ugly American in me. I need to check my motivation for this trip.

I wish I could call my AA sponsor. He didn't think I should come back here.

The cabbie asks "Can you get tickets for me and my wife? The ride will be free"

"I'll see what I can do--write down your name and number."

We roll up to the front of Carolina's building and the driver retrieves my garment bag and backpack from the trunk.

In an overly smiley instant, he gives me his information, vigorously shakes my hand and waves. I press a twenty into his palm, knowing I have no intention of getting him tickets. What a shitty way to return to this lovely place! Sometimes I hate myself for what I can be.

I need a drink.

Part Eight: DRINK

"I have missed you so, so much, my RRRrrrrobert," Carolina whispers in my ear, rolling her "r's" as we embrace for the first time in over a year.

It feels very warm and sexy, but extremely awkward. In an instant, I know I don't share her sentiment. The fire in me is gone. This feels really flat.

"I've missed you too, baby," I lie.

Carolina reaches down the front of my jeans, kisses me deeply and says, "I am going to have a shower, you may want to clean up too."

"In there," she points to her guest room.

"We will have a private party tonight. Just the two of us," she wiggles out of her skirt and turns towards her bathroom.

I must look like a deer in the headlights.

We still had an appreciation for each other's physical skills. In a few hours we were napping, exhausted from our sweat-drenched reunion.

We awaken at about nine p.m. and Carolina immediately heads to the liquor cabinet and pours herself a rum and coke. She stops by the fridge and whips out a Heineken for me. Before I can say anything, she opens it and pours it seductively into a frosted pilsner glass. The curves of the glass, sweating from cold and heat, resemble Carolina's shapely body and the caramel color was like her skin.

"No thanks, I'm not drinking today." I tremble as I push the glass away.

"But you are here now, baby. No one will know." She says.

I take her hand in mine and look her directly in the eyes, saying "I can't drink Carolina. It will kill me."

"You are being so dramatic, my Gringo. Maybe you should move here and I'll train you to be a great alcoholic actor!" She chides me.

Not content to sit in a beautiful condo overlooking the historic Spanish citadel on the bay, she grabs her car keys, throws to me and says, Okay, good, you can be my designated driver!"

Part Nine: DRIVER

We spent most of the evening at a nightclub accompanied by almost everyone involved in Carolina's new show. Although she didn't try to force drinks on me, Carolina made a point to announce several times that I was sober. No shit. The only one in the party who was anywhere near as straight as me was an elderly catholic nun who volunteered at the theater, and she tossed back some kind of smelly red sangria all night. I offered to take her for a tattoo, but she politely declined.

The party escalated, the singers sang and the dancers danced. I felt like I walked onto an overexposed Fellini set.

Somewhere around three a.m. I carried Carolina's semi-conscious body across the condo lobby, up the elevator, and poured her into bed.

My heart was pounding and my hands shook so much I could hardly write:

Dear Carolina:

Thank you for inviting me back to your lovely island.

I am not the man you knew previously. I am not the person I once was. I am now living a sober and thoughtful life, full of hope and optimism.

I wish the same for you.

If I stay here with you I will probably begin drinking again. For me, to drink is to die. My choice is made, and I choose life.

I will leave your car at the airport in the short term parking lot, with the keys under the gas tank lid. I will also leave some cash under the floor mat to help compensate you for the expense you incurred to bring me down here.

Carolina, you are a beautiful, sexy, and talented woman, who would fulfill most men's dreams. I am, unfortunately, not that man.

Wishing you love and light in your life.

Break a leg.

With love, Robert

I drove to the airport in San Juan at four in the morning.

Randall picked me up at LAX.

I am approaching my twentieth-fourth year of sobriety and Carolina has not called or written, or reached out in any way.

I saw her on YouTube recently, accepting a music award.

She looked pretty happy without me.

INTAKE

I am sitting on a cold, steel, battleship gray folding chair. It backs up to a sterile green wall, outside a long row of office doors. The floor is so well-polished I can see my distorted reflection. From this point of view I look very strange, like the image in a fun house mirror.

But this is no fun.

It is December, 1989 and I am in my Navy Dress Blues. It has never been a comfortable uniform to wear. It is made of stiff, scratchy wool, and there are thirteen buttons securing a flap where other men simply have a zipped fly. There is a right way, a wrong way, and the Navy way, and apparently the Navy way involves a rigorous procedure to take a piss.

Which, as usual I have to do when I'm nervous.

My traditional uniform is sharp and crisp, adorned with the shiny medals and ribbons of a sailor who has been in the fleet and performed well. For a First Class Petty Officer, my achievements are considered outstanding.

Until now.

Behind the office door, the future of my nine-year Navy career is being discussed by a physician, two counselors and the Command Master Chief of my unit.

Two men and two women. My poor judgement with a junior enlisted woman is the reason for this party.

I don't expect much sympathy.

Recently separated, and deflecting court orders and threats originating from my ex-wife's camp in Philadelphia, I have taken drunken refuge with a young female sailor. Not a good career move, as this particular woman happened to be my direct military subordinate. The current chain-of-command has a real problem with fraternization. Add to this indiscretion the fact that all this has taken place at the very Naval Air Station where the notorious Tail Hook sex scandal has just played out, and one can see why my little fling has embarrassed the entire station.

Bad timing.

The door opens and I snap up from my seat to a position of attention. It is the Master Chief and without a word she points her finger at me and motions to come into the room.

I briskly take three steps into the room, come to attention and announce:

"Petty Officer McClellan reporting as ordered Ma'am!"

I'm facing the female doctor, who is also the commanding officer of the Naval Hospital.

"Good afternoon, Petty Officer, have a seat," she responds.

"We will proceed informally, as this is a medical board, not a Captain's Mast."

"Understood?"

"Yes Captain," I say, leaping to my feet.

Addressing such a senior commanding officer from a sitting position can't help my case, I think.

"Sit, and stay seated McClellan," the Master Chief explains, "You have permission to be at ease."

She nods towards the seat. Her tone is almost soothing. I am beginning to sense that this may not be the lynching I deserve. But I still have to pee and I am scared shitless.

The Captain turns the meeting over to Dave, one of the two civilian counselors. He is extraordinarily tall and thin, with pale, almost translucent white skin. He is a strange looking man who obviously dyes his inky black hair.

"Robert, are you an alcoholic?" Dave asks.

His eyes are clear and icy blue. He looks directly at me and I feel his powerful inquiry shooting right to the darkest places in my heart.

The honesty of his question catches me off guard. I am accustomed to people beating around the bush about such things. I sit and wonder what is his ulterior motive.

I don't like Dave.

The second counselor, Charlie, picks up the thread, "Do you consider yourself an alcoholic, Robert?"

There is something disconcerting about being in my full dress uniform with all the "I love me" ribbons and medals festooned on my chest, and being addressed by my first name.

I am shaking.

"Err, um, I don't know," I stammer.

"I've never really thought about it, I guess."

Which is pure bullshit because I think about it every waking moment, except it usually sounds like: "What the hell is wrong with me?"

"This is a simple question, my friend," says Dave, in a calm voice that sounds like it could have originated in a deep icy cave.

"Are you, Robert, an alcoholic?"

I turn and look at the Master Chief. She stands silently blocking the door, and nods her head once in my direction. I am trying to interpret what it is she wants me to say.

I know this moment is important, yet I am paralyzed by fear.

I squirm and look for help in the faces that confront me.

"If I knew how to answer that question, I'd probably not have to be here."

The Captain leans back in her chair, disengaging. She is running out of patience.

"Ma'am, I am probably considered an alcoholic, I guess, by some people," I addressed the Captain.

"I didn't ask you, Petty Officer McClellan," she said, leaning forward and pointing across the room, "I believe these gentlemen did."

Worrying silently, I knew I was out of options. I reeled her back in, but now she's tossed it back to the cold, calculating counselor, who already knows the answer to his own question.

"Okay, I am an alcoholic!" I blurt out.

"I am an alcoholic and probably a drug addict and a shit load of other things too!"

I loudly poured it out onto the floor in a rare moment of honesty.

Suddenly, the tension disappeared from the room. It was as if someone had opened a window and all the bullshit and lies of a lifetime were sucked outside.

No one said anything. I was losing the battle to buck up and not sob.

Dave rose from his chair, stood towering beside me and put his hand on my shoulder.

"Captain," he said, "I believe this young sailor is worth our efforts."

"Agreed," she said, "We are finished here Master Chief."

The Master Chief handed me some tissues and said, "Get yourself squared away." She led me out the door and down the hallway to a conference room.

Closing the door behind her, she stood in front of me and grabbed me in a warm embrace. I felt weird being hugged by my Master Chief.

"My name is Cheryl, and I'm an alcoholic," she said.

"Welcome to the rest of your life, Robert!"

I didn't know what to do. I wasn't really a hugger. My arms went limp.

Awkwardly, I excused myself to go to the head. I peed, sat down and cried.

People believed in me when I least deserved it.

DRUGGY BUGGY

The Druggy Buggy pulls up to the dark loading dock behind the Naval Hospital.

Is it really necessary to hide us from public view, next to the dumpster garbage and medical waste, as we board the conspicuous white van that transports us to local A. A. meetings?

This is just one of dozens of new resentments I will embrace over the course of my three month inpatient alcoholism treatment.

Counselors told me that I'd free myself from a lifetime of fabricated fears and anxieties, which triggered my addiction. They failed to inform me that I'd discover new people, places, and things on which to hang the responsibility for my shortcomings. Beginning with them, the professionals and counseling staff that seemed so interested in my well-being, I made brand new shit lists, identifying my latest detractors and enemies.

Wheezing and coughing in smoky A.A. meeting rooms, I secretly hate the weak fuckers who can't even put down the cigarettes and let the rest of us breathe for an hour. All the while, I constantly run back to the coffee pot, hide in the men's room, and stand outside demanding some fresh air. Any excuse not have to sit in those ass numbing folding chairs and listen to the speakers.

I might accidentally hear something I could use in my own life, and would have to stop blaming everyone else in the world for my drinking and drugging.

After an agonizingly long hour, I line up with the others and get the meeting chairman to sign my attendance card.

Some of my hospital mates are smiling and happy, and discussing the topics of the meeting. I am trying to be invisible, sitting in the back staring out the dirty window of the van.

Before I got sober, I always thought that it would be a very long, painful, and complicated process. (Because I turned everything in my life into a long, painful, complicated process; it only made sense that such an important undertaking would be the most tricky and convoluted thing I've ever done.) Soon after accepting sobriety as a way of life, I discovered what a simple, uncomplicated solution this was:

Don't drink.

Go to meetings.

Pray.

Talk to my sponsor.

Repeat.

As I did these simple things, day after day, things got better. My life moved slowly from darkness to light.

Sometimes agonizingly slow and steadily towards a promising, happy future.

I learned to get out of my own way and allow people who cared for me to become a part of my life. I learned to humble myself and ask for help. Not easy for someone like me, who thinks he is the smartest guy in the room, needs no one, and prefers to isolate with the person he admires most: himself.

But there is all this new A.A. program jargon, all the secret handshakes and all the steps and traditions to learn. There is a huge textbook to study. Surely, to be sober I must complete and pass the exam in the back of the book, right?

Wrong. Wrong on every account.

There are no secrets. Everything, all the knowledge and all the love, is freely given with no strings attached. And the only test is the one that I take on a daily basis.

Did I stay sober? Yes!

Did I love another? Yes!

Did I engage my Higher Power? Yes!

Did I make myself available to anyone who reached out for help? Yes!

Pass! Go to the head of the class.

Guess what?

Same exam.

Same time.

Tomorrow.

And tomorrow is not guaranteed.

DANIEL

Every Thursday evening, our treatment center group attends the A.A. meeting at a local high school. A classroom is set aside, and volunteers rearrange the desks to accommodate our larger adult frames. A tall wooden cabinet is wheeled in and placed by the door, and several stained coffee pots and stacks of Styrofoam cups are piled on top.

To my amazement, smoking is permitted in the classroom's last two rows.

There are always several group members assigned to be greeters, and they welcome everyone with an enthusiastic, "Hi my name is - welcome to the group."

A bit too enthusiastic and smiley if you ask me.

They seem a hair's breadth removed from the creepy Pentecostal church ushers, eager to hang up your coat, then reappear midway through the service with a wicker basket, asking for "love offerings."

There is a member of this group that I've considered asking to be my A.A. sponsor.

His name is Dan, he's in his sixties, a retired sailor with a few spars loose. When he speaks at the meetings, half the room thinks he's from another planet, while the rest hail him as a profound philosopher. I think he is bat shit crazy, but I also appreciate and find great encouragement in his pearls of recovery wisdom. He has been sober more than twelve years now, and when he speaks of his drinking days, he reminds me of myself. He's my kind of guy: a former hard drinking Navy man with a bit of a wet brain.

I've been coming to this meeting for about five weeks in a row, enough time to size up some of the regulars.

There's a long haired heavy metal dude named Kenny who likes to bring up smoking weed every time he is called on by the chairperson. Some of the Old Timers groan loudly and get up for coffee, but they allow him to finish. Another guy named Dave wears too much cologne and seems to be here to pick up women. He always ends his sharing with an emotional, over the top, insincere message of gratitude to his Lord and Savior, Jesus Christ. I don't ever sit near Dave, preferring to avoid the Almighty's inevitable lightning-bolt throwing wrath. I think I'm allergic to his musky scent. Dave's, not the Almighty's.

There are a few women in the group, mostly middle aged and very emotionally fragile. One older gal called New York Nancy, however, is hard as nails, and makes it very clear that she is no wilting daisy. She swears like a Teamster and takes pride in making the other girls blush as she shares war stories of her drinking days in the Bronx. The younger girls are attracted to her and the older ones avoid her like the plague. She sponsors a handful of newcomers, women she calls "my pigeons." If men were permitted to pick female sponsors, I'd be asking Nancy to be my mentor. It is no wonder that Dan and Nancy are the best of friends.

There are dozens of edgy characters at this meeting, mostly irreverent types who wholeheartedly embrace A.A.'s tradition of non-governance. There is only one Authority in A.A., a personal Higher Power as you choose to express it. This group embraces just enough anarchy for me to become comfortable here. I think I'll ask Dan to be my sponsor.

After the meeting, I corner Dan over by the coffee pots. He is cleaning up the meeting's mess while engaged in two or three conversations at once. He is a smiley red-faced, white-haired Irishman, with a booming laugh. His blue eyes are clear and intelligent. Standing around and listening, I detect that there is much more to Dan than his space alien persona. He seems to genuinely care for this Fellowship, and carries the message of hope to his brother alcoholics.

As Dan locks up the cabinet, and we are finally alone, I say, "I really like what you have to say, and wondered if you'd be my sponsor?"

Handing him a folded piece of paper with my phone number on it, I say,"maybe you can call me sometime, and we can go to some meetings together."

Asking for help has never been one of my stronger traits.

Dan unfolds the paper and studies it for a moment. Laughing, he crumples it up and tosses it into the coffee cup filled wastebasket. He looks me in the eye, and I feel stupid.

Reaching out with both his strong gnarly hands he grasps me by the shoulders and squares me up to his six-foot two frame.

"Listen Bobby, I don't need your number. I already know how to get drunk," he says. "If you want to know how to get sober, then you call me every morning at ten o'clock, starting tomorrow."

He doesn't waver. He continues locked on my eyes. He squeezes the back of my neck and asks, "Got it?"

Dumbfounded and unable to break his laser beam stare, I say, "okay, but I don't have your telephone number."

He releases his grip, turns for the door and says, "Well, if you want to stay sober you'll figure out how to get it."

He is gone before I retuned with a pencil and paper.

New York Nancy sees me in distress and comes over. "Gonna be Danny's new pigeon?" she asks.

"I think so," I say.

"Well don't just think, do! Your best thinking is what got you here!"

She said, "Just call him and do everything he asks you to do. Don't drink, call your sponsor, come to meetings, and pray. A lot. That's all you need to know to stay sober right now."

Nancy grabs the pencil and reaches into the wastebasket, recovering the crumpled paper I handed to Dan. She writes Dan's phone number on it.

"C'mon," she says. "I'm taking you to the Village Inn for ice cream."

"You'll be my excuse for a chocolate sundae."

Fast forward: Dan and Nancy have both passed over before their time.

Sober.

I picked the right space man.

DOC COWBOY

This is the day I get to meet my new doctor.

Not as a patient, (that would come later) but as a nurse. I'm working the old green-tiled hallways of the V.A. Hospital in the Black Hills of South Dakota. Most of our patients on this twelve bed ward are Vietnam era Native American men. Lakota warriors who were sold out by their government in a never ending pattern of broken promises. This is the last promise, a deal they made with the United States to be taken care of in their waning years.

The Indians are losing the battle again.

The constant budget cuts and politicization of the Veteran's Administration has all but incapacitated our ability to provide for the basic needs of these humble men. They don't ask for much. They demand nothing. They just want the dignity of a comfortable death.

The new Doc is something of a legend in the Black Hills. He is a World War II Marine Corps veteran of the Pacific. He was present at Iwo Jima. A small town Wyoming boy, working his way through adolescence on the rough and tumble ranches near Casper when the Japanese bombed Pearl Harbor, he answered his country's call. Claiming to be eighteen and a bit tall for his age, he enlisted in Cheyenne. A Bronze Star and a Purple Heart later, he used his GI Bill to get through the University of Wyoming Medical School.

Practicing as a physician in Rapid City for forty-five years, he rose to be the Medical Director, President and CEO of the large regional medical center. He lived a simple life on a small ranch with his wife and daughters. Their old stone house had no air conditioning and was heated by a fireplace and a wood stove. Not many healthcare CEO's were splitting wood and training cutting horses on their days off. The Doc never took a single golf swing in his life. He preferred to swing an axe, or ride alone into the sacred Black Hills and camp along a stream with his dark chocolate trail horse.

The Doc's wife died just two years into his medical center retirement. Both his daughters had become physicians and took positions in Denver. He got lonely (if such a thing is possible for cowboys) and decided to go back to work. Today is his first day as the resident doctor on our ward. We are happy to have him, because the last two physicians were very young men and they didn't quite relate to the older veteran patients. (One of them, a good doctor, was, ironically, Vietnamese, and the vets didn't give him much respect.) The young docs certainly had a hard time understanding the unique Lakota culture, and the mix of traditional and allopathic medicine in the Native community. Some of the older nurses know Doctor Cowboy and he has treated some of their family members.

At our shift report, the nursing supervisor introduced Doctor Cowboy to the staff. He is a lanky, hard, tanned man, with thick white hair. It is difficult to tell if he is eighty or fifty years old. Under his white lab coat he wears a starched denim shirt, open at the collar. I've been told that he hasn't worn a proper necktie since the day he was married. When asked if he'd like to address the nursing staff, he looked at the Supervisor and said, "Well Mary, I'm just hoping you and the nurses can keep an eye on me and don't let me make too many rookie mistakes." He smiled warmly, nodded at the charge nurse and headed out to the ward where he grabbed some charts and started seeing patients.

I caught up to him as he headed into my patient's rooms. "Let me know if I can help, Doctor," I said.

Doctor Cowboy nodded, but kept his attention on the patient. He asked the man a few questions about his diabetes, looked his chart, and scribbled down some notes in the medical record. Tossing the chart to me, he said, "I don't do so well with computers, so I'll write my orders and you can enter them into the system for me. I'll sign them when you print a hard copy." I caught the chart and replied "Yes Sir." The Doctor looked at the large Native American man in the bed, and asked him what his rank was when he was in the service. The Indian veteran

replied, "I was a Staff Sergeant, 101st Airborne, Sir."
Then the doctor turned to me and asked, "Are you a veteran?" I said, "Yes Sir. Petty Officer First Class in the
Navy SeaBees." Doctor Cowboy squeezed my shoulder
and said."Well, you both out rank me. I was a Marine
Corporal when the war ended, my parents were married,
and I've always worked for a living. I haven't earned the
right to be called sir by servicemen."

Wow! This guy is different.

As a "quasi-military" organization, most of the V.A.
Doctors insisted on deferential treatment and as many
honorific titles they could squeeze out of the staff in the
course of a work day.

Over the next year, Doctor Cowboy and I enjoyed a
close working relationship. Often times we were the
only male staff members on the ward, and that certainly
accounts in part for our congeniality. But, most importantly to me, he was a genuinely kind, down to earth
physician, who cared for his patients and always made
me feel like I was an equal partner of the treatment team
taking care of his people. Ironically, at one point I became his patient after a nasty gout attack. He warned me
that I was drinking too much coffee, eating too many
sweets, and if I cut it out, my gout attacks would subside. Of course, he was downing a huge cup of Joe and
wiping cake icing from his face when he offered that
advice through a huge sarcastic smile.

On a snowy November Saturday afternoon, we were in our staff meeting preparing to take over the evening shift when Mary told us that Doctor Cowboy had been thrown from a horse and had some kind of head injury. The ambulance crew from Wyoming tried to take him to the big emergency room in Rapid City, but he convinced them to bring him to our small V.A. hospital. The nurse practitioner in the E.R. dressed his wounds, but noticed his cognition was compromised and he kept losing his balance. Despite his protests, she had him transferred by helicopter to the very medical center of which he was once the boss.

Later in the shift we got word that the doctor was in surgery. He suffered a subdural hematoma and was bleeding on the surface of his brain. They had to drill a hole in his skull to relieve the pressure. His prognosis was guarded and he was going to be in the hospital for a while.

We got a temporary doctor from another V.A. to cover all of Doctor Cowboy's patients. It didn't look like our old doc was going to return to work any time soon.

On my day off, I went up to Rapid City to visit Dr. Cowboy. He was in a nice private room in the rehab department. As I entered his room, he sat in the big bedside chair with a bandaged head and one side of his beautiful white hair shaven down to the scalp. His eyes were bruised and bloodshot. He looked like he had been in an old Western saloon fight. There was a tray with his lunch on it. He seemed to have nibbled on a few pieces of chicken and ate the crackers, but most of the lunch was untouched.

I walked over to him. He still did not acknowledge my presence. He stared blankly at the television, which was tuned to some game show channel.

"Hey Doc!" I said. "How they treating you up here?"

"Hunh?" was his reply. "Joseph? Where's Gloria?"

I was startled. Maybe he was medicated and didn't recognize me. We worked together five days a week, so I'm sure he knows me. This was disturbing.

"Doctor, its Robert. From the Hot Springs V.A. I'm a nurse on your Med-Surg Ward," I said.

"Joseph, get Gloria. Someone is stealing our diesel," was his reply. "Call Gloria!"

I said, "Okay, I'll go get Gloria. Here, I brought you something." I placed a big slice of chocolate cake on the tray beside his uneaten lunch. I took his big, sinewy hand and put a fork in it. He was still as strong as ever and he squeezed my hand with just a hazy hint of recognition and acceptance. His eyes cleared up, then just as quickly, they glazed over again.

I walked out of the room fighting back tears.

Doctor Cowboy never returned to work.

Although I don't ride, I've fallen from plenty of horses.

PURGE

There are dozens of boxes.

The cardboard repository of my memories.

Containing neatly labeled photographs, newspaper clippings, badges, trophies and medals, they are insignificant way stations, on an excursion long ago abandoned.

I build a small stone fire pit in the back yard. The Buddhist practice of detachment comes to mind, and the Ceremony begins.

One by one, hour after hour, I hold these worthless treasures in my hands and drop them into the flames. I give them, and all the moments they represent, to the Universe. My heart sinks a bit when I see the framed print of my loyal, departed Irish Setter, crumpled up and licked by the flames. His smiley dog face melts away, and for a minute I question whether this is a good idea.

The smoke rises into the crisp South Dakota night. I assign some flaw, some character defect, to every floating ember, racing upward to join the clear, starry sky. There is absolution. I forgive myself for my shortcomings as the ashes glow and the morning arrives.

This is the first light of my new life.

CHRIST, TENDERIZED

I hate waiting in lines. Or as my lovely wife calls it, on queue. Whatever you call it, it sucks. I used to say that I wouldn't wait in line to see Jesus riding a bicycle. Perhaps I have learned a bit of patience in my middle age, for here I am, in line, queued up to see a movie about the crucifixion of Jesus, Mel Gibson's "The Passion of the Christ."

About ten minutes into the film, I thought that ol' Mel should have changed the title to "The Tenderizing of the Christ." For the entire long opening sequence, we are treated to the graphic, sweaty, bile spitting flogging of Jesus of Nazareth. Up close and personal, he is depicted suffering for our sins. I was flinching as he was flailing.

Now, Gibson has always been a controversial character regarding his faith. He reportedly belongs to a tiny cult within the catholic church that practices a very narrow philosophy that outside the church, there is no salvation. He has even been quoted saying that his own wife, although a much better person than he, cannot get into Heaven because she is an Episcopalian. He has also been accused of being an anti-Semitic drunk. "The Passion" certainly hung much of the blame for Christ's suffering on the Jews. Gibson's version has the Romans doing the dirty work at the behest of the local Jewish leaders.

I struggled through the screening. It was really a terrible piece of film making, no matter what one's religious beliefs may be. As a person raised and educated in the Roman Catholic tradition, I found it disturbing and heavily sadistic. I'm told that the movie stuck pretty closely to the Catholic account of Christ's crucifixion. The film reminded me of my own struggles with the validity of the Catholic scriptures. There is a whole other conversation we could explore about what gospels are accurate, and which are included in various versions of the Bible. Most people are unaware that, over the centuries, many accounts of the life of Jesus did not make the various edits and cuts to the accepted, authorized, King James Bible. There are said to be about fifty-two texts written by prophets, spiritual leaders, and perhaps Jesus himself, that have never made it into any standard Christian denomination's official canon. Remarkable, yet not surprising. We wouldn't want to upset the gravy train that has become American Christianity, now would we?

As the theater owners counted the night's box office receipts, the train of dazed viewers leaving from Gibson's movie led directly to a small storefront, a few doors away from the lobby. In a leased real estate office, an army of Christian Counselors was standing by to console the flock. The counselors, who were purported to be volunteers of various denominations, were in fact, trained recruiters from the Southern Baptist Convention.

They travelled all over the state, following the "Passion of the Christ" as it made its way into the hinterlands. The irony here is that the Baptists, particularly of the Southern variety, consider Catholics like Mel Gibson to be the spawn of the Anti-Christ. But that never got in the way of a good opportunity to recruit new souls for the cause.

Onward, Christian soldiers!

In the counseling office, there was a lady, rocking back and forth, her eyes rolled back into her head, uncontrollably weeping and chanting, "Help me Jesus, help me Jesus…" Another younger girl, maybe fifteen years old, was allowing an older gentleman counselor to lay his hands on her and drive out Satan. In many Pentecostal traditions, the laying on of hands is a gift from the Holy Spirit, reserved for only the most worthy, (usually male) practitioners. The counselor would sharply smack the youngster's forehead and yell, "Be gone! In the name of Jesus Christ, get behind me Satan!" The teenager cried and cried, and her black eye makeup ran down her cheeks. She looked a lot like my old posters of rock music demon Alice Cooper. The counselor raised the stakes. He began slapping the girl on the back and bending her over backwards. It was like a scene from "The Exorcist." I half expected the young girls head to turn around backwards on her neck. She shook convulsively and I decided I had seen enough of this bizarre religious sideshow.

I dropped two dollars in the donation jar as I hit the exit door, springing back outside, and into the fresh air of rational sensibility.

There is a tremendous difference between religion and spirituality.

I really have no use for religion.

I will just be that direct with these fanatics. When they launch into their religious pitch, I will ask them, "what makes you think my spiritual path is inferior to yours?"

My great friend, (and first A.A. sponsor) took a very direct approach when members would invoke the name of Jesus during meetings. Alcoholics Anonymous does not subscribe to any particular religious belief, and people are free to choose whichever Higher Power works in their lives. But it is a personal choice and discussing issues of religion and politics are avoided and frowned upon by most A.A. groups. When a certain arrogant member of our group took to quoting scripture and calling upon his Lord Jesus during his time to speak, my sponsor would yell out, in his gravelly voice from the back of the room, "Hey, if your good buddy Jesus isn't a stinking drunk, he doesn't belong in my God damned A.A. Meeting!"

I am now many years sober.

Not a single day can be attributed to Jesus Christ.

LAZY

I can be a lazy slob.

The most ambitious thing I may do today is shave. And, if I wasn't concerned about appearing somewhat human for my wife, I'd probably sit here all day surfing the web, occasionally interrupted by writing a few uninspired paragraphs, and growing a beard down to my chest. I'm pretty sure a long, scraggly, pasta-stained beard would qualify as a bio-hazard, so I'll eventually make my way into the bathroom and shave. Fear of infestation beats lazy every time.

I've been fearful of many things. Mostly afraid of relationships blowing up in my face. I've always had this irrational feeling that everything and everyone good that comes my way is undeserved. Scared that my lesser nature would reveal itself in a relationship and the girl would leave me. And the fear was well founded because I've lost my share of nice girlfriends and a few nicer wives along the way. Even though I appear to be extremely confident and secure, there is always the chance that I will sabotage every positive life situation.

Maybe it is restlessness. Maybe it is a deeper psychological deficiency that causes me to recall my mother's physical and verbal abuse towards me when I was a child. Maybe I'm raw meat for Jung and Freud. Maybe I'm just a narcissistic asshole who can never be satisfied.

At this point I enjoy a lifestyle that I've only ever dreamed of achieving. I have a remarkable, accomplished wife. My job is creative and independent and it allows me to work from home. My health is good and I have many recreational opportunities right outside my door. I have friends all over the world, and along with my wife, we travel and explore the planet. But, I am having a real problem appreciating it all.

I've been in recovery from alcoholism for over two decades.

I've studied Buddhism and practiced yoga. I've been to Lakota sweat lodges. I've been baptized, circumcised, and *psychedelicized.* Most of these spiritual pursuits have disappointed me. Or, maybe I'm just too lazy and skeptical to commit entirely to the spiritual experience.

I think I'll just go shave.

ERIC

It is two in the morning and I am sitting with Eric Taylor on my worn brown leather couch. We are totally engaged in a heated debate over the death penalty.

Eric is one of America's most profound songwriters. For thirty years he has been recording and performing critically acclaimed music and has a well-earned reputation as an outspoken individual. Taylor is an eloquent communicator and may be the one English speaker on the planet for whom the word "fuck" was invented. He has fine-tuned its proper use and drops it into his arguments as effectively as a hand grenade. It is not so much profane, as beautifully appropriate, coming from him.

Taylor strongly believes that some people, child molesters for example, simply need to die. On the other hand, I don't think the State should be in the business of killing people for any reason. The government can't even operate the motor vehicles department efficiently, let alone administer swift capital justice. We are strong willed guys on opposite sides of this issue.

Jill, my Canadian wife, sits across the room and soaks up both sides of this white-hot debate. She is far too civilized and well mannered to engage us. And watching this robust argument must be intriguing to her.

Eric has played an intimate private concert for us tonight. It is my fiftieth and Jill's forty-second birthday party. We had about sixty people seated on the covered back deck, listening to every note of his colorful, character-driven songs.

Eric Taylor's tunes are like your grandmother's fine china that has been accidentally dropped, broken and then lovingly glued back together. Like the adhesive, his songs get on you and can't be easily scrubbed off. Authentic prose, set to beautifully minimal virtuoso guitar playing, Taylor's songs come from a lifetime of gritty experiences. He is a man of the road, playing music everywhere, with almost everyone. Classified as a "Texas" musician, he has written songs that have been recorded by artists as diverse as Lyle Lovett and Joan Baez. Like Guy Clark and Townes van Zandt before him, you can taste the dry dust on your tongue as he unravels each gripping narrative. Perhaps Eric Taylor is living a few centuries too late, as he is surely the kindred of the traveling Renaissance troubadours. His descriptive song introductions are as mesmerizing as the tunes that follow. When he shares his story of learning the blues from "Pegleg" Arthur Jackson, it isn't because, like most white artists, he studied and listened to everything that Jackson ever recorded. He is intimate with Pegleg's music because as a young man Taylor sought him out and as circumstances unfolded, they wound up living in a 1951 Chevrolet sedan together, Jackson sleeping in the back, Taylor up front. Arthur Jackson worked the Southern sideshow minstrel circuit, and Taylor had nowhere else to go, so he drove Pegleg around and learned what the Blues smells like.

Sitting here in this cozy Florida living room, a million miles from, and a lifetime beyond that '51 Chevy, softly sipping a glass of red wine and hammering home his thoroughly researched and unwavering opinions on war, politics and the sad plight of the American Indian, Eric Taylor fills the room with his cognitive power and charm. I am once again in the undeserved company of a tormented genius.

This is what problem intellect looks like.

Knowing I served in the military during wartime, I suspect that he is curious about my pacifist stance.

"Killing is killing," I insistently say.

Red-faced and with his black beret at a radical tilt, he refutes me with statistics and examples of the most violent and gruesome acts forced upon young girls by their sadistic killers, offering me a chance to change my mind.

I don't.

Jill looks over at us and I sense her fascination and I think to myself that she has probably never been in the company of such passionate and outwardly tough, yet inwardly sensitive men. She occasionally joins the conversation, offering clarity and civility when our wheels start drifting over the edge.

The next morning the three of us muster in the living room, shaking off cobwebs, drinking coffee and bumping into furniture.

Taylor is packing up his green guitar case into the road weary white pickup parked in the gravel driveway. He is preparing to drive to his next gig in south Florida.

Jill rises and warmly hugs him as he steps toward the door.

Eric gives her a boyish smile and his eyes soften a bit.

"I was laying in bed thinking that maybe I shouldn't come right out and say that some people should just die…!"

Whatever pain or frustration buttressed his previous argument, melted away as she kissed his cheek.

There are 374 inmates on death row in my home state of Florida.

The number awaiting execution in Taylor's Texas is 391.

In Ontario, Jill's Canadian home, there are exactly zero.

To listen to Eric Taylor's soulful songs visit:
www.BlueRubyMusic.com

RASTA BUDDHA

It is a prematurely gray and wet summer afternoon in Manhattan. The wind is blowing sheets of rain sideways, claiming dozens of cheap umbrellas. Brightly colored women dart from office buildings, splashing through greasy puddles in three hundred dollar shoes, diving into the open doors of steamy taxicabs. Jill and I take refuge at the Borders coffee shop in the Time Warner building.

As she finds a restroom, I order two soy mochas from a middle-aged, handsome, Jamaican man with the softest brown eyes I have ever seen. He is training a younger, darker, troubled soul with a heavy Nigerian accent. The African man's stormy demeanor mirrors the weather. As they work the cash register together, I step up to pay for the drinks. The younger employee is having difficulty mastering the computer-based system and can't make correct change. The older fellow attempts to help.

"You're making me angry!" the frustrated trainee snaps.

"No, little brother," the Jamaican gently replies, "I can't make you anything…your anger has roots in your heart."

Telling them to keep the change, I intercept my wind-blown wife. Embracing her, I spy an empty café table.

"The Buddha works the coffee counter, " I say.

MY NEW DEAD FRIENDS

Ron. Mark. Horst. Carl. Tim. Wes. Agnes. Xavier. Carlos…

These are my new dead friends.

My wife, Jill, worked with, trained, or was a colleague to them. She is not a cop, fire fighter, or soldier.

She is a cave diver.

So were they.

Recently, I produced a documentary about a scuba diver who went missing in a Florida cave. I narrated the film, and said:

"Cave diving is sometimes referred to as the world's most dangerous sport."

This simple statement created a shit storm of controversy among the cave diving community, and I was challenged and vilified on Internet diving forums for making such a bold claim.

I have been a soldier, a sailor, and a prison medic. In all my years in these dangerous roles, I never lost eight acquaintances. In the past seven years married to Jill, I came to know every one of these people, and grieved their premature deaths.

Every one of these remarkable people were, in some way making the world a better place.

I am now becoming hard-hearted towards Jill's newest dive buddies, students and associates.

I don't want to hold Jill, as together we write your obituary and cry at your passing. I love you too much to like you.

COLONEL

January 20, 2009, 12:15 p.m.

His long, angular brown face is crowned with a neatly groomed shock of closely cropped white hair. The sofa on which he sits is too low for his height, and his lanky legs, with bent knees, are splayed outward in front of him. Cream colored argyle socks complement his spit shined G.I. oxfords.

Pinned to the collar of his yellow windbreaker is the eagle device of a full-bird Army colonel. Over his heart is an American flag pin and a miniature silver star medal.

In the far corner lobby of the Lake City V.A. Medical Center, sits a huge flat-screened television. Gathered around are dozens of people. Some are medical and janitorial staff, others are patients with canes, wheelchairs and walkers. All are transfixed by the crisp high definition image from the steps of the United States Capitol.

It is solemnly quiet. The only sound is the whoosh of the automatic door sliding open and closed.

All eyes are riveted on the TV.

On the screen is a handsome young African-American man, his right hand raised and his left hand resting on Abraham Lincoln's personal Bible.

The white-haired warrior on the sofa buries his face into his knobby, arthritic hands, and quietly sobs.

He reaches over to me, sitting on the metal chair to his right. He squeezes my arm and cups my hand in his weather beaten leather grasp.

He leans closer.

"Eighty-one years," he says in a hoarse whisper.

"Eighty-one years I fought for this...I prayed for this day"

I clasp his hands firmly.

With tearful eyes we sit there, two veterans weeping.

Mission accomplished, Colonel.

NINE ELEVEN

He took a bullet in the head.

Just above his left eye, a gaping wound exposed a mangled skull, with jagged bone fragments and soft, wet, pink brain tissue. The great jihadist mastermind, Osama bin Laden, the proclaimed enemy of the United States, is dead. Perhaps the most influential man of our time, Bin Laden and I were born in the same year.

Baby Boomers.

Brothers from different mothers.

Another one bites the dust.

He will no longer terrorize the fitful sleep of those who lost loved-ones on September 11, 2001. He will no longer release chilling videos and threatening audio tapes, promising to strike America again.

Yesterday afternoon, a U.S. Navy SEAL commando plunged a stake through the heart of Islamic evil incarnate. The soles of the SEAL team's boots tracked his sticky blood through his Pakistani safe house. As they gathered computers, hard drives, and other intelligence from his sanctuary, Osama's children and wives knelt cowering in the courtyard, zip-tied hands secured behind them, expecting to be executed. But, these stealthy operators are quiet American professionals. These are America's twenty-first century warriors. They are not sadistic seventh-century al Qaeda or Taliban barbarians. The raid was over, and the women and children were left for the local authorities to sort out.

Rewind to a clear September Day:

Almost every person I know can recall exactly what they were doing at 8:46 a.m., when American Airlines Flight 11 was crashed into the World Trade Center's North Tower, followed by United Airlines Flight 175, which hit the South Tower just seventeen minutes later. Like the Kennedy assassination and Neil Armstrong's first step onto the moon, the moment is frozen in time.

I was a world away, in the peaceful, early morning sunshine of eastern Montana. A tall, thin woman was showing me some property, just outside a little whistle stop cow town. The hub of a classic western ranching area, Terry, Montana is the antithesis of the hectic eastern cities in which I had been living. The wheels had fallen off my marriage, my nursing career was unfulfilling, and I was considering a fresh start in the clean air and wide open spaces of Big Sky country. I was interested in buying a small country cabin, a former rancher's bunkhouse, just outside town. It seemed like a very sweet deal because, for the price of the house, it came with an adjoining property: The Pioneer Drive-In movie theater. A tarnished, funky, nineteen sixties style drive-in, the Pioneer was right up my alley. At several points in my life, I've worked around motion pictures. My first real job was assistant manager of the Crest Theater, in Philadelphia. This led to an opportunity with Paramount Pictures branch distribution office, where I was a film booking clerk. A few years down the line, I took over the booking and programming of the Theater of the Living Arts, a revered repertory cinema on Philly's famous South Street. I loved movies and I was beginning to love Montana. It seemed like a great fit. It was exciting to be on the cusp of this new chapter in my life.

I could not close the deal until I returned to St. Augustine and settled things with my disconnected, disinterested wife, Liz. We were clearly on different wavelengths, and had agreed to part ways when the best opportunity presented itself. Liz and I decided that when we encountered the next fork in life's road, we'd choose separate paths. We liked, even admired each other, but the passion was gone. In my early forties, I was not yet willing to live in a sex free marriage. Perhaps in another forty years, when I was in an adult diaper and mindlessly whizzing around in a wheel chair, but not now. Liz was fit, sexy, and in a classic hippie chick way, quite beautiful. There was s time when we had a lustful attraction to each other, driving ourselves to sweaty simultaneous orgasms.

Then, after she returned from her three month writing sabbatical in Mexico, she just became aloof and unresponsive.

We tried. But it was flat and emotionless. I became frustrated and resentful. What could have happened in Mexico to change her sexual attitude into this unapproachable ice queen? Liz swore it wasn't anything I had done, she just claimed to have evolved spiritually beyond the need for physical sexual satisfaction. She was a remarkable Yogini and took her practice very seriously. I was at a loss. Some of my purest tantric experiences were sexual.

It was stressful and sad.

The Realtor and I headed back to her office on Main Street, where I'd write a check for a deposit on the property. I really wanted it. I could see myself there, running a drive-in and becoming a Big Sky space cowboy.

Driving back towards town, we talked about movies and how to resurrect the dusty old drive-in theater. Life seemed brighter now, and my world was full of great potential. We stopped at the Rancher's Co-op for gas.

Like many small agricultural communities, the grain elevator is also a general store, gas station and rumor mill. The Terry Rancher's Co-op was like a scene from an old John Ford western film. There were even tumbleweeds blowing across the gas islands as we filled up. I thought it looked very cinematic. Suddenly, everything was being processed as famous Hollywood scenes by my over eager, movie obsessed brain. The gas pumps were right out of "Five Easy Pieces." The Co-op was from James Dean's "Giant."

I held the door against the wind as my Realtor, Carol, swept into the old brick building to pay for her gas. As my eyes adjusted to the dim interior, I could make out dozens of antlered bucks mounted proudly from the rough wooden rafters above. Every spare inch of wall space had some stuffed creature's eyes staring down at the Co-op's big stone counter. Heads of deer, elk, bison, mountain lions and bears, all preserved and peering out from their wooden perches. There were the usual few aisles of necessities, and shelves full of candy and chips. A big glass freezer held soft drinks, fresh buffalo steaks and live bait. No one was manning the store's cash register. There were about a dozen men in the back room, gathered around a few sparse tables, watching an ancient portable color television, balanced on an overhead plank, high in the corner between a decrepit VCR and some type of dusty bowling trophy. It was a news bulletin, a special report. CNN's Aaron Brown was on the split screen. He seemed distressed. There were some buildings on fire. Big skyscraper buildings in New York.

"Carol, have you heard?" asked an overexcited plump lady in an apron.

"Heard what? No, I've been out showing property."

"Oh my God, honey! Someone attacked New York!"

"The World Trade Center."

A leathery, white whiskered old geezer in a cowboy hat chimed in.

"Hijacked some airplanes and crashed 'em smack into it. Never seen anything like it, just collapsed into the damn street. Just fell the hell down, they did."

His clear, sparkling blue eyes had surely seen a lot of things, and the surreal scene playing out on the TV above him was beyond belief.

My eyes were now riveted on the modest screen above the corner table. Anxious news correspondents were breathlessly checking in with the latest updates. And then I saw it plainly for the first time: the airliners approaching, then disappearing, then crashing into the upper floors of the towers! Then, after burning a few minutes, the towers fell. It was inconceivable. Again and again it played, as Aaron Brown threw the coverage to reporters in the field. They speculated, guessed and theorized what may be going on in New York. Hundreds of police, firefighters and medics rushed through the choking, disintegrated concrete, dispatched to an address that no longer existed. The towers had fallen. First one, then the other, crashing in on themselves in clouds of eery gray smoke and debris. The detritus of high finance and international trade floated down on lower Manhattan. Papers, folders, files, gracefully descended from 110 stories high. Memos from the heavens, sent by people who are now dust in the autumn wind.

Then I saw the footage of falling people.

Desperate people in blowing skirts and business suits were clinging to the thin edges of windowsills before the buildings crumbled. With smoke and flames licking at them from the interior, some made the decision to jump. It was hard to watch. A woman took off her high heeled shoes, brushed off the soot from her business jacket, buttoned it, and holding her shoes in her hand, dived from a tiny ledge. There was a dark-skinned man with a long white cloth, maybe his office curtain, waving it over his head, signaling for some miracle rescue from unseen angels circling above. Then, clutching the white material with both hands above his head, he jumps, perhaps hoping it will become like a parachute and break his fall. Suddenly he is falling face forward, arms flailing and kicking his legs. He loses a black shoe. Releasing the fabric, he disappears behind another building, sparing me from witnessing his body hitting the street.

Hoping I will awaken from this nightmare to discover it is only a Bruce Willis blockbuster thriller, I am slowly, reluctantly, absorbing the grim reality of a new America.

The small group of locals who meet at the Co-op for coffee and conversation is taken aback. There are involuntary "Oh my God's" and "I can't believe it's" as they watch, almost stunned. One of the oldest men has his gnarled hand wrapped around a crushed styrofoam coffee cup, and appears to be on the verge of sobbing. Another fellow's cup has teeth marks worked around the edges in neat, nervous rows. These are real men. Real cowboys, real ranchers. Most of them have been to war in Korea or Vietnam. They can't seem to summon the appropriate emotion, so they opt for stoic silence.

Or anger.

They step outside two at a time, fire up a smoke and engage in a red faced, animated conversation.

The TV coverage continues with reports that now, the Pentagon has been hit. CNN switches between New York and Washington D.C. as the situation becomes more confusing and dynamic.

"That's it!" says one cowboy. "This is war!"

"With who?" says his buddy.

Bin Laden and al Qaeda were not yet seared into the public consciousness, but by day's end, there were a lot of fingers pointing towards Afghanistan.

All I wanted to do at this moment was hear Liz's voice.

I asked Realtor Carol if she was doing okay.

"I'm shocked." was her reply "but OK I guess. I need to get home and find out what's happening with my kids at school."

We drove back to her office parking lot, listening to the news coverage on the radio. It was on every station, across the dial. They reported that President Bush was in a safe location and the federal government was intact and in charge. The military was on a high level of alert. Air traffic was being grounded, and planes in the air were being diverted to the nearest city where they could safely land. The authorities encouraged calm, and asked Americans to pray. Carol sped through town, ignoring stop signs. I prayed that we would not get in a car wreck.

Thanking Carol for showing me the property, I reached out to shake her hand. She took my hand and pulled me in to a tight, warm, boney embrace.

"It is time for a hug, now."

"Yeah, and go hug your kids, too. We'll figure out this drive-in deal after things have settled down."

I hopped in my old red Ford pick up (pick up trucks are oddly called "outfits" in Montana), and headed to I-94 towards Miles City.

I was finishing up a thirteen week travel nursing contract at a small hospital, and only had a few more shifts left before I could return to Florida. There was very little traffic on the Interstate. I looked up and noticed two fighter jets screaming high in the Montana sky. There are dozens of air bases and ballistic missile sites in this part of the country. As a military veteran, something deep inside me involuntarily whispered aloud "Go get' em boys!"

I was staying at a small railroad hotel in Miles City's historic district. The place was neat and clean, and offered efficiency apartments by the month. Most of the guests were itinerant construction and railroad workers, and people like me, who were doing some kind of contract work. Many rural western towns could not staff their healthcare facilities with permanent, home grown nurses and therapists, so there was a revolving door of temporary talent keeping the hospital up and running. I depended on these small town nursing gigs, and they paid me obscenely well to work the overnight emergency department shifts. It was a good arrangement, allowing me to travel, escape my perplexing marriage, and call my own shots.

But right now, I wanted to call my estranged wife.

"Liz!" "Are you alright?"

"Yes, I think so, I'm shaken up, but trying to stick to my routine."

Liz was a writer and yoga instructor. She had a small studio in the cottage behind our house.

"I've decided to go ahead with my class this evening. I called my students and most of them want to come."

"Good," I said. "It may be best to just stay in the groove."

"I have tonight off, but I'm going to volunteer to cover any ER shifts if the local staff want to stay home with their families."

Strained as it was, our relationship was always kind and friendly. I cared deeply for Liz, and she for me. We ruined a great friendship with a shitty marriage.

"Robert, I'm afraid here. There are jet planes everywhere, and helicopters flying really low down the river."

"It's okay Liz. They're from NAS Jax. I'm sure there's an alert. They probably sent the carriers out to sea and the planes are flying out to land on them. It's how the Navy does things…"

"Well, they're loud, and low, and they scare the hell out of me and the dog."

We had Cory, a rescued greyhound. He freaks out during thunderstorms and whines like a baby. I'm sure the jets were making him insane.

"Just be glad they are up there, Liz. This thing may not be over."

"I had to turn the TV off. It is just too ugly for me. I went out to the studio with Cory and cried. What kind of animals have people turned into?"

"When are you coming home Robert?'

"In about a week and a half. I have four more shifts scheduled and then I have to drive. Maybe I can leave a few days early if I can get someone to cover my last shift. Just relax, Liz, I know you are hypersensitive and an empath, but don't get this all over yourself."

"Okay, well, I've got to get ready for my students. Maybe a yoga session will help to balance the universe."

"Alright, take it easy. I'll be home as soon as possible. I'll call you from the hospital tomorrow night. I Love…"

"Bye."

Click.

That's it.

Bye.

Click.

No "I love you," or any other affectionate phrase. Although she didn't mean it, I would have like to have heard it. I guess it felt good to know that she was okay. Even with all the problems we faced with our marriage, Liz was the only immediate family I had. Our intimacy was borne of habit and necessity. Neither of us were close to our parents or siblings. She was the only true confidant I had. I could be myself, show my weaknesses and celebrate my strengths, knowing she would not judge me. Man, if only she could get her sexual fires lit again, we'd be awesome! At least the memories of sex with Liz comforted me, as I lay alone in a small hotel room watching the rest of the world fall apart, live on every channel. No one, it seems, would ever be the same.

I fell asleep.

There was a soft knock on my hotel room door. I scrambled up, found some scrub pants and looked out the peep hole. It was Toni, another traveler who worked at the hospital. She was a bright, young, Asian-American respiratory therapist from Denver.

"Hi Rob, I hope I'm not bothering you."

"No, I was just laying around watching the news on about five channels at once. I think I broke the remote."

"Yeah, me too," Toni said. "Gee, I wondered if you wanted to order a pizza or something. I just don't want to sit around in this stupid hotel eating dinner alone."

"Sure." I said.

"Let me get cleaned up and you order it. I like everything but pineapple on pizza."

"Whoever thought of putting fruit on a pizza?" She laughed. "That's gross! I bet they weren't Japanese. We just put raw fish on ours. We put raw fish on everything. Okay, meet me at my room."

The last thing I remember about September 11, 2001, was Toni's head resting on my chest, as she drifted off to sleep at the end of the longest day in many of our lives. Her dark bangs framed her angelic, porcelain face. Her leg curled over mine, and her skin was softer than anyone's I had ever touched. My head was devising dozens of seductive scenarios, but my heart said, no, she is a frightened young girl who came to me for friendship and comfort. We were refugees, clinging to the safe haven of human touch.

A week later, I made the long drive from Montana, home to Florida. All along the way, I wrestled with my decision to buy the drive-in theater. I desperately wanted a new start, a fresh chance to be happy and healthy.

But my conscience burned a hole in my plans.

I had to stay with Liz. Protect her from this suddenly tumultuous and uncertain world. However, my sense of duty and loyalty were not shared. Liz and I were soon divorced. My dream of a quirky Montana drive-In faded, as the world woke up at war and held its breath, waiting for the next catastrophic color-coded terrorist attack.

We were all bit players, thrust into a Tom Clancy screenplay…

Osama bin Laden had three wives. All were present at his death.

One of them took a bullet, attempting to shield him from the Navy SEALS who came to deliver us from evil.

Amen.

COLD DEAD FINGERS

I am surrounded by guns.

In the rural area of North Florida where I live it is normal to hear gunshots every single day. People hunt on the open acreage adjoining my property. Half way down my gravel driveway, a quarter mile from my house, is a thirty-acre lime stone pit. This pit has been used for generations of shooters as an impromptu gun range.

I don't flinch when I hear rounds going off at any hour of the day or night.

You know that scene that pops up in country music videos?

The one with a half dozen pickup trucks and a bunch of cowboy booted, shiny young country people drinking Bud Lite around a bonfire? With the guy in a Real Tree ball cap is leaning over the shoulder of his hot bikini-topped girlfriend - helping her to fire his deer rifle at the beer can targets set up at the edge of the party?

That's the pit next to my house.

From just the sound, I can usually determine the caliber and type of guns being discharged down there.

I own firearms.

I have a state issued concealed carry permit.

I served in the military and earned expert pistol and rifleman awards.

I know guns. There is a pistol in the drawer beside my desk as I type this.

And - I am a supporter of tighter gun control and regulation.

What?

How in the world can a guy with several guns want more gun control?

Newtown. Aurora. Virginia Tech. Columbine. Tucson. Santa Barbara. Las Vegas.

My heart has been broken.

I've changed.

How can we accept that these place names are now interchangeable with mass murder gun tragedies? My mind is made up. We can no longer afford to ignore the terminal cancer in our society.

In each of these tragic events the shooters should never have been permitted to be near a loaded weapon. But, because firearms are so easy to obtain, so easy to buy without detailed and thorough background checks, the mass murderers succeeded in ruthlessly killing and maiming innocents.

It is time for this nation to take a clear and sober look at the violent culture that has arisen over the past few decades. And, because it seems that there can be no reasonable debate or discourse when it comes to the subject of the Holy American Gun, the Federal government will be pressured to act decisively.

But will it?

Some of my friends and neighbors are what could be called Preppers.

When you live in a farming county where storms, hurricanes and even wayward raccoons on power transformers can cause blackouts lasting days at a time, preparation is a prudent step. I have extra food, water and fuel here on my ten acres. I have a stand-alone LP gas generator wired into my house's electrical panel. I plant a fairly large vegetable garden surrounded by banana and fruit trees. I'm prepared. But what sets me apart from my Prepper neighbors is that I don't have a weapons arsenal.

They do.

They believe the shit is about to hit the fan.

And many others truly believe that before this happens, the government will attempt to forcefully confiscate their firearms.

I've discussed this situation at great length with these friends and neighbors. Here, in abbreviated form, is the synopsis:

1. The New World Order crowd will deliberately implode the U.S. economy.

2. Society will break down. First in the cities, then the rural counties. The city dwellers will form mobs and in great hordes they will come to the country seeking to rob us and steal our water, food and weaponry.

3. Somewhere in this apocalyptic scenario, the Federal government will declare martial law and round up all the so-called "Patriots" to be sent to FEMA re-education camps. Troops will comb the countryside looking for resisters and and shoot armed citizens on sight.

4. Only the armed resistance will have a chance to survive and start the New American Republic.

That may sound a lot like a "Red Dawn" movie script, but it is the blueprint for the near future held by many people that are close to me.

None of whom, by the way, have ever served a day in the actual armed forces.

I ask them what they plan to do when an Abrams main battle tank rolls into the horse pasture next to their house.

The consensus is that "at least I would die fighting."

There's something pathological at work here. The fear in their eyes is evident when this conversation comes around. It is a collective type of Paranoia.

Will this be a self-fulfilling prophecy?

"Love Thy Neighbor as Thyself..."

No.

"Fear Thy Neighbor…"

RELIGIOSITY

"Do not believe in anything simply because you have heard it. Do not believe in anything simply because it is spoken and rumored by many. Do not believe in anything simply because it is found written in your religious books. Do not believe in anything merely on the authority of your teachers and elders. Do not believe in traditions because they have been handed down for many generations. But after observation and analysis, when you find that anything agrees with reason and is conducive to the good and benefit of one and all, then accept it and live up to it."

- Siddhārtha Gautama Buddha

The two women stood staring into a giant dairy case at the Winn-Dixie in High Springs, Florida. The case was stocked from top to bottom with a diverse selection of milk alternatives. There was soy milk, almond milk, vanilla soy, rice milk, chocolate almond, coconut, and more. The ladies were about my age, maybe a little younger. With simple, ankle length prairie dresses and long hair pulled into severe buns on top of their heads, the pair looked a bit out of place in 21st century Florida. For a moment I thought they may have arrived here via a time warp. Put them in an old Hollywood western movie, sitting in the third pew as the preacher conjures up fire and brimstone from the oaken pulpit, and they'd look perfectly natural. But mesmerized by the bright lights of the milk section, they were dumbfounded.

"Excuse me ladies, I just want to grab some almond milk."

I reached beyond them and picked up the half-gallon carton. They stared at the boxed milk as I placed it in my cart.

One of them, with a round collared white blouse sporting a huge gold cross, lowered her eyes and asked me, "What kind of milk is that?"

I picked it back up and showed it to them, "Almond milk. For people who don't drink cow milk. But I don't know how they can get way down there and milk those tiny little almonds."

Blank zombie stares.

"It's really great in coffee, you should try it."

The younger woman makes steely eyed contact now, sternly narrowing her gaze. "Oh, well, Pastor John does not permit us to drink coffee."

I smile, tip my ball cap, and pause as I begin to turn away.

"Oh cool, just like the Taliban."

The nineteenth century women shuffle down the aisle to the cheese section, where they seem more comfortable.

Pastor John of the No Coffee For You Church, Pastor Terry Jones of the Koran Burning Dove Outreach, Pastor Fred Phelps of the God Hates Fags Congregation in Wichita, and Pastor Harold Camping of the World Will End on May 21st But Didn't Cult, are all symptoms of a very disturbing reality in current American Christianity: Controlling, egomaniacal preachers preying on the ignorant and weak.

HAPPY BIRTHDAY

Today is my 50th birthday.

I am up to my elbows in an inmate's blood.

His five lacerations are self-inflicted. One of them nicked the brachial vein, too deep to stop with direct pressure.

Puddled on the floor beneath the chair to which my patient is shackled is a half-liter of dark, sticky, coagulated blood. Doing some fancy dancing, I avoid stepping in it.

A twenty-five-year-old, light-skinned, black man, with blood smeared on his face and body, he looks like a character from a slasher movie. I inform him he is probably not going to die but is being sent to the emergency room to be sutured. Showing his gratitude, he spits in my direction. His blood-tinged sputum lands on the floor in front of me.

Happy Birthday.

I am a nurse working in the medical department of a hard core Florida prison. This is the one where the Department of Corrections houses death row inmates until they are hustled into a nondescript white van and driven next-door to be executed.

My assignment tonight is the Crisis Stabilization Unit.

CSU is a politically correct name for the psych ward. The administration seems to prefer sending male nurses here. They say the inmates are less likely to act out when a physically imposing man is at the medical station. The administrators need to come out of their offices and walk the wings once in a while. Some of these inmates live for the chance to intimidate male staff members.

Most of these offenders are serving long sentences. More than half will never be going home. Classification as a psychiatric patient removes an inmate from the general population. It is a very effective way to be housed away from other inmates who want to rape and stab you. As prison life goes, CSU is a relatively safe place.

Once they are admitted to CSU, their security status changes from a closely guarded, dangerous convict, to a loosely guarded, dangerous mental health patient. Great for the inmate, no so much for the medical staff.

Inmates can be professional manipulators who know the legal limits of the system. On psych units they don't have to work, and can't be gassed, pepper sprayed or disciplined by the correctional officers. The nurses check on them at least once an hour.

So, even though the inmate may have raped or murdered someone to get to prison, he's not considered a security risk on CSU. He's now just another behavioral health case with a thick mental health chart.

And on the CSU, he's not accountable to the security officers and staff.

He's suddenly my responsibility.

Cutting one's self is one of the quickest way for an inmate to earn a CSU cell.

They ingeniously acquire objects with which to slash their forearms. If the staff knew how easily inmates could access sharp objects, they might never come to work again. Prisoners use sharps and shanks on themselves (and each other) with regularity.

Those who self-mutilate are called "cutters."

For maximum shock value, some cutters tie off their arms with a piece of cloth, creating a downstream tourniquet. When the pressure is suddenly released, venous blood squirts across the room. To the novice staff member it appears to be an arterial bleed, requiring urgent intervention. Since the inmate is behind a locked steel door, and the inexperienced nurse can't get to him, this causes great chaos.

Prisoners thrive on chaos.

The officers charge in, extract the bleeding victim, and the inmates on the wing get a free show. The wounds rarely need more than a few butterfly closures and some gauze dressings.

End result? The inmate has successfully alleviated his boredom and earned additional time on CSU.

The rest of my evening passes quietly.

The cutter I sent to the E.R. has returned with some fresh sutures and all the activity seems to have tired him out. He sleeps through the next pill pass. All of these inmates are prescribed heavy doses of antipsychotic medications. About a third of them refuse to take their meds. It is a game they play to remain in the care of psychiatrists. Each refusal requires more and more documentation. This is just what I need: more paperwork.

During the last round of the evening, I speak to a young inmate. Convicted as a juvenile, with only four months left of his juvie sentence, he turned eighteen and was transferred to this adult prison. He is housed here in CSU for his own protection. If he were placed in the general population this likable, bright teenaged boy would certainly be attacked and raped.

Prison is a culture of predators and prey.

Happy Birthday.

My shift ends. I turn in the personal body alarm, keys and medical access badge at the control station. The steel gate clanks securely behind me and I am greeted by the crisp January night. Above the parking lot, in a clear star-filled sky, the constellation Orion shines down. He has always been a good omen. I slowly drive out of the lot, turn left onto the highway, and the eerie illumination of the prison fades in my rearview mirror.

Arriving home, I take a baptismal shower and slide between the clean sheets of a very welcoming bed. Holding my wife's soft, warm body, I spoon her, squeezing firmly.

Lying in this peaceful place, I imagine how different life would be if I was held accountable for bad choices I made in my youth.

Burying my nose in the nape of her neck, I drift to sleep looking forward to the next fifty years.

Happy Birthday.

THE JANITOR

Mopping up the blood.

For some reason I am stuck on the image of the poor guy who has the task of mopping up the blood of innocents after the latest mass shooting.

Like cleaning spilled milk from the cafeteria floor, he mops, rinses, squeegees, mops, rinses, squeegees. The water turns a ferrous shade of deep red in the yellow plastic bucket. "Caution! Wet Floors" is etched into the side of the small orange safety cone the man has placed near the doorway.

In the corners, he must get down on his knees and, in a full-body plastic suit, he uses a small sponge to patiently soak up the blood from the room's crevices. His shoes are covered with hazmat boots and he tries not to step in the sticky, congealed lifeblood of the massacred.

He stops every few minutes to remove his safety glasses, and with a moist paper towel, wipe his watery eyes.

There is no hazmat protection for his heart.

"For this is my blood of the new testament, which is shed for many for the remission of sins."

Matthew 26-28

REAL SOBRIETY

At twenty, I knew I needed to get sober.

Crammed into two warp-speed decades was a lifetime's worth of decadence, frustration, and disappointment. I cheated death, avoided jail, and escaped serious injury and disfigurement.

I embraced sin, greed and conspicuous self-indulgence.

Only a deeply suppressed belief that I could be someone better than the damaged young man staring back at me in the mirror, kept me moving forward. Two steps forward, one step back, at a time.

I was a seeker, fighting the faint notion, the distant possibility that there was a complete and satisfying life for me.

If only I could stop drinking and drugging.

I wasn't ready to make that journey.

I wasn't finished sabotaging my success and happiness.

Time flies.

There were three marriages.

Two children.

Four houses.

One gun in my mouth.

Countless wrecked cars.

A dozen jobs.

Scores of disappointed family, friends, and mentors.

Thousands of beers, and innumerable lines of coke and crystal meth.

I'm not even bothering to count the acid, pot, and pills.

There are tattoos, reminders that are not worth removing.

The measure of years is significant. The journey that is my recovery began when I was thirty-three years old. I am now fifty-seven, and recently noted my twenty-fourth year free of drugs and alcohol.

Somewhere, early in my first year of sobriety, I knew I wasn't going back. As hard as it was to remain clean and sober, I couldn't stand to be that demented man again. I am a pussy and couldn't live through the pain and misery of another detox and recovery.

This book is my best defense from myself.

To view the documentary film go to: RealSobriety.com

Topics for Book Club Discussion

1. In "Epiphany," the author recalls the moment of clarity when he decided he needed to quit drinking. Have you ever experienced a pivotal moment in life when you wanted to change everything?

2. The theme of "It wasn't supposed to be like this" can be interpreted as the author's disappointment with his generation's misplaced priorities at the dawn of the twenty first century. Do you think that the realities of your life lived up to the expectations you had as a younger person?

3. In "Vietnam" the author describes the first time he recalled his community experiencing the personal loss of a serviceman during wartime. Have you or your community experienced the loss of a loved one or friend from military service? Did it change the way you felt about sending young people to serve in the military? Do you think that we should consider mandatory service for young people?

4. The Baby Boomer Generation considers the assassination of President Kennedy to be the moment

when America lost its innocence. Almost every Baby Boomer could tell you where they were when those shots rang out in Dallas. Which experiences in your lifetime created the same shared emotional experience - when everyone could tell you precisely where they were?

5. In "Jack" the author had a profound supernatural experience. Do you believe in spiritual communication after death? Have you had a similar experience to the author?

6. In "Repo" the author is brutally honest about his use of cocaine and his inability to manage his life. Do you think people should be open about destructive behaviors from their past or should recovering addicts and alcoholics be more discreet?

7. In "The Steps" the writer describes his first visit to an AA meeting. Throughout the book, he recounts periods of recovery and relapse from substance abuse. Do you think relapse is part of the journey out of alcoholism? Do you think an alcoholic or addict is ever "cured" of their affliction? Is addiction a moral failing or a disease?

8. As a young man, the author worked alongside famous artists as a concert stage manager. Who is the most famous person you have ever rubbed elbows with?

9. Doc Cowboy left a powerful impression on the author as an older mentor and "fully formed man." His accident changed their relationship. Have you ever experienced a similar loss when an injury or illness caused the dynamics of your relationship with someone to change dramatically?

10. The chapter titled "Eric" examines capital punishment in America. What are your thoughts about the death penalty? Do you believe that there are still some crimes that should be punished with death? Should minimum or maximum sentences be placed on perpetrators of specific crimes? Does the prison system need reform?

11. The author describes the stress he feels about losing new friends from SCUBA diving accidents, and that he worries about his wife whose job puts her in the face of those same dangers every day. His relationship with his wife is a role reversal from what we normally see in society. Wives of firefighters or

policemen face similar stresses as they wait for their spouse to come home each day. Do you think the author should bravely accept the fear of losing his wife to her occupation? Is it different for women that wait for soldiers, electrical linemen or public safety workers to come home?

12. Where were you when the Twin Towers fell? How has your life changed since 9/11?

13. There are several parts of the book where religion is treated with irreverence. The author appears skeptical based on his personal experiences with organized religion and yet many of his anecdotes reveal his spiritual sensitivity. Can spirituality exist without religion?

Interview with the Author

What was the impetus for writing this book?

I think that for whatever reason, I have been gifted with a remarkably interesting life. I have an inner drive to tell stories and share experiences with people. A good part of what I am trying to accomplish is to try to stimulate conversations and cause the reader to have a reaction - good or bad using my own life as a template.

Did you ever worry that your wife would be shocked or disappointed when she read about some of the early episodes of your life?

Which wife?

Oh sorry... yes... I have felt sensitive to how people I care about would react to these stories and revelations. But my wife Jill, has actually been my muse. Telling these stories has been cathartic. She has been completely non-judgmental about my past and has reminded me over and again that the man I am responsible for is the one I am today not the man I was thirty years ago. We all come into relationships with some sort of baggage, whether it is previous romantic baggage, professional issues, or emotional stuff. It is what makes us human. You can't get to your forties or fifties and start a new relationship and not realize that there has been a lifetime of experiences that included ups and down. It is all about accepting the person you are today and forgiving yourself for the person you used to be.

As a Catholic boy I was taught that I was born with the original sin of Adam and Eve. As soon as we get smacked in the ass, we have baggage to account for. It has been a long road towards forgiveness for me, when I finally decided to stop letting that baggage weigh me down.

If you could go back and whisper in the ear of the young man who was cast out on the streets of Philadelphia by his own mother, what would you tell him?

I would tell him that he has value and that he is worthy and has dignity. I would tell him that he has nothing but a giant ball of potential to do great things in the world but he is going to have to work hard and overcome his humble beginnings and dysfunctional family. None of it will come easy but it is worth persevering.

What advice would you offer a young man growing up today?

Wow… I almost feel like that is my life's mission. I would say, "don't be afraid to explore your boundaries.

Don't accept other people's limitations or expectations of yourself." There has never been a better time to be a young person and we are at the dawn of a new age… a new society that is based on sharing and technology. Technology gives them a lot of tools. Happiness is not necessarily a fat bank account or a flashy car. There has never been a time previously when so much was possible. "Continue to constantly improve yourself and gather knowledge and skills and stand up for yourself. Don't be a pussy. Get off the tit." And as my father said, "at all costs, be a gentleman."

What do you want to work on in life, either literally or figuratively?

I have an intellectual curiosity that is almost a curse. I am always looking to learn new things whether it is in the field of history, technology… or anything. I am always seeking.

Like a lot of guys my age, since I left the military I have been slowly getting out of shape. I would like to work on my physical fitness and general health. I want to work towards getting fit enough to participate in a competitive sport again.

I tend to isolate myself and I would like to work on relationships. I want to nurture more equitable relationships with my friends where I can just be of service to them rather than just finding what they can do for me.

More than anything though, I will use my Dad's advice to find a way to work with my brain rather than my body. I love writing and have a lot more stories to tell.

Has your writing allowed you to discover things about yourself and your past that you never considered before?

Oh yeah... there is a lot of this stuff in this book that was buried very deep. As I started write, one thing led to another. I would recall a situation with a person and then I would question, "do I really want to talk about this? Do I really want to go here?" I spent a lot of time trying to move on from being a drunk or an addict or a cheat or a fraud and I wasn't sure if I wanted to go there to relive it again. It was my life though. They were the choices I made. It still hurts to relive some of those situations especially the ones that hurt other people. I was very self destructive, but I was blind to the collateral damage of my self destruction for much of my life. I have three ex-wives and two estranged children. I have had about fifteen different jobs. Somewhere along the line, people got hurt. I wish I could go back and soften that stuff a little. I wish I could have lived a full life without hurting anyone, but I didn't. Perhaps writing about it all, the good

and the bad, is part of my healing. I am learning to forgive myself, but I don't necessarily think that everyone I
hurt will be able to get there too.

What's next in writing projects?

Volume Two is well under way and volumes beyond
that are bursting to get out. I have a drawer full of unfin-
ished fiction as well and I am excited about having the
time to bring those to fruition. My wife and I are com-
pleting a book about our journey across Canada by bicycle. It should be very unique as we volley it back and
forth discussing the best and worst of incredibly challenging conditions on the greatest and most intimate
journey of my life. My ultimate goal is that someday I
will have one of my screenplays produced for the big
screen.

This book was produced
by Heinerth Productions Inc.

Contact them for help with your
publishing project at:
JillHeinerth@mac.com

www.ingramcontent.com/pod-product-compliance
Lightning Source LLC
Chambersburg PA
CBHW052135170626
46812CB00004B/1421